8 MIRACULOUS ENERGIZERS TO TAP INTO

When the Troops are Tired!

David R. Mains

MAINSTAY CHURCH RESOURCES
WHEATON, ILLINOIS

WHEN THE TROOPS ARE TIRED
Copyright © 1997 by David R. Mains

Cover art: Joe Van Severen
Book design: Blum Graphic Design
Editor: Nancy Gruben
Printed in the United States of America

07 06 05 04 03 02 01 99 98 97   10 9 8 7 6 5 4 3 2 1

ISBN: 1-57849-044-8

To tired staff members

who time and again

have gone above and beyond

in their service for the Lord.

CONTENTS

Introduction

1 *Finding Tension's Good Side* 1

2 *The 24/7 Church* 19

3 *Christian Hospitality* 39

4 *Pulpit/Pew Mutual Support* 59

5 *Prayer with Fasting* 79

6 *Telling Our Stories* 99

7 *The Wider Kingship* 121

8 *The Living Christ* 141

FATIGUED

by Greg Asimakoupoulos

Battle weary.
Bleary eyed.
I'm tired of the fight, Lord.
No wonder I'm wearing fatigues.
Your name may be hallowed,
but my heart rings hollow these days.
My will is done
before your kingdom's come with power.
Our enemy advances
thinking his chances
of victory improved.
Prove him wrong, General Jesus.
Reinforce your troops.
Begin with me.
Renew my will to win.

I was embarrassed to the point of making an executive order that the Chapel van not be used anymore. Then it broke down on Chicago's Eisenhower Expressway and had to be towed to the nearest garage. The mechanic who looked it over said it would take a miracle to get the van running again.

Shiny red when we first purchased it, we had the Chapel Ministries logo painted in white on both sides. And the truth is that it served us well for quite a number of years. But by the end of its tour of active duty this vehicle had a number of combat scars. To save costs we had done some of our own repair work, and I admit the replacement parts didn't always match in color or style.

What really bugged me, however, was the van's boldly printed proclamation under the logo, which read, "Dedicated to the vitality of the local church." That's how we define ourselves as a ministry. But I fear anyone who read those words as we drove by would be forced to conclude that the body of Christ was in big trouble. Our van's battered appearance implied that if this was where help was coming from, things were bad for the church indeed.

For the present, one of my employees is using his own van to carry out Chapel assignments. It looks pretty good, but I haven't had the nerve to request that something about vitality and the local church be painted on its side.

In the months that followed our vehicle's demise, I started to forget my earlier sense of embarrassment. Knowing it was no longer on the road, I could laugh when old Chapel van stories surfaced at coffee breaks. Still, there lingered in my mind this haunting question of whether our "clunker" in some ways represented a certain kind of reality. *What about your church, Lord?* I wondered. *Are your troops tired, battered, scarred, on their last legs? Would it take a miracle to get them running again?*

> THERE LINGERED IN MY MIND THIS HAUNTING QUESTION OF WHETHER OUR "CLUNKER" IN SOME WAYS REPRESENTED REALITY.

What God's people actually feel about the state of the church is determined to a large degree by the health of the congregations in which they've participated. The truth is, there are marvelous churches in every state and province. It's also a fact that many other congregations are really struggling.

Church attendance in America is on the decline. According to William Hendricks in his book *Exit Interviews: Revealing Stories of Why People Are Leaving the Church,* nearly 7,600 people are leaving the church in Europe and North America every single day. He writes,

> That means that every week, more than 53,000 people leave church and never come back. To put that in perspective, consider that the United States lost about 57,500 people in the Vietnam War. . . . Or look at it another way: a "large" church is said to be one that has 1,000 people attending each Sunday. We would have to plant at least 7 1/2 large churches *every day of*

the year to offset the number of people walking away from churches we already have. (p. 252)

According to Hendrick's figures, 2,700,000 people are leaving the church in Europe and North America every year.

Indeed, I seem to meet more and more of these people. Ask the simple question: Where do you folks go to church? Listen to the hemming and hawing. Then discover that these Christians don't really go to church anywhere. They've given up on church because of old wounds or because "church just isn't relevant to real life."

Though we hear much about the phenomonon of the megachurch, the average size of most congregations is 107 people. Indeed, George Barna in *User Friendly Churches* says, "The vast majority of Christian churches in America are either stagnant or declining in size. Relatively few of the nation's 300,000-plus Protestant congregations are increasing the number of people who attend their worship services by at least 10 percent each year "(p. 15). Similar studies in Canada reveal additional dismal figures. *Less than 8 percent of all churches in America are growing more than 10 percent per year.*

In addition, surveys suggest younger generations are not being reached by today's churches. According to Mike Regele in his book, *Death of the Church,* who reports on the results of a 1993 demographic study of churches, "While the face of America is changing, for the most part the face of most large historic Protestant denominations is not, except for the color of members' hair! "(p. 107). He goes on to cite that persons seventy years of age and up are significantly above the national average for the United

Methodist, Presbyterian (U.S.A.), and Evangelical Lutheran churches. Persons between fifty-two and sixty-nine are above the national average in each of the denominations. Persons between thirty-four and fifty-one (boomers) are below the national average for the above denominations as well as for the Southern Baptist church. And persons between thirteen and thirty-three are significantly below the national average among every denominational group except the Southern Baptists, and they are still below the national average.

Regele concludes from all this: "Across all denominations, there is a failure to reach the youngest generation.... In other words, while the overall U.S. population is graying, *the historic Protestant insititutions are graying faster!* ... Based on demographics alone, the future of the church is grim" (pp. 107, 109).

Does it sound like the troops are tired? Without the vitality and enthusiasm of younger generations infusing us with fresh concepts and new dreams, what is the hope for the future? Church experts unilaterally agree that something drastic needs to happen soon to reverse these trends.

Perhaps another telling way to evaluate the overall state of the church is to ask what impact Christianity is having on our culture. From that perspective, most North American Christians would agree that the present church doesn't begin to influence society the way the early church did. A miniscule number of Americans are reading God's Word each day according to Barna Research and the Gallup Poll. These pollsters also agree that there are no discernible differences in the behavior patterns of Christians and non-Christians.

Yes, if we assume a more global view, the picture improves. For example, in parts of Asia today, the church is alive and attractively aggressive. In certain sections of Africa or Central and South America, believers don't look all that unlike their New Testament counterparts.

But in the States and Canada, far too many things compete with a vibrant faith. We're more caught up in a thousand other activities like making money, keeping in shape, chauffeuring kids, watching television, getting counseling, landscaping the new house, repairing the old house, working toward a degree, following sports, entertaining friends, practicing with the quartet, surfing the Internet, reading the newspaper, shopping for groceries, developing marketable skills, holding the family together.... Most believers don't have the time or the energy to consider the "state of the church." But in this culture it's not just non-Christians who are pooped trying to keep up with everyday life.

Don't misunderstand. Christians are concerned that our society appears to be coming apart at the seams; but for most of us, the shootings, the drugs, the vandals haven't affected us personally all that much. These distresses are items on the evening news or in the daily newspaper—somebody else's problem, in somebody else's neighborhood. The gradual national decline and the ineffectiveness of Christians to halt that descent only affects us in incremental ways.

Is the faith a priority for most church people? If we are honest, we probably answer: Not to the degree that it should be.

Do Christians in North America have a way to go before they match the standard set by their New Testament brothers and sisters? Sometimes preachers look at what used to be through tinted glasses. They tend to see only what was good and conveniently overlook the bad. Even so, doesn't the Bible report it was said of the early church that it turned the world upside down? That's quite an accomplishment! I think we must admit we are far from this in actuality.

Do people in the pulpit and the pew still see the miracle of New Testament Christianity as a viable option in North America? Understanding global issues the way we do, we know Christians have put their faith on the line in China or Eastern Europe, in Uganda and Bolivia. But do any of these sacrifices have all that much relevance to us on the North American continent?

> IS THE FAITH A PRIORITY FOR MOST CHURCH PEOPLE? NOT TO THE DEGREE THAT IT SHOULD BE.

Anyway, no more questions right now, please. We prefer not to have to think all that much about such big topics. Besides, we need some time to pay bills, to buy a new outfit, to make an important phone call, to take the dog to the vet, to get a hair cut, to fill out tax forms, to drive the *family* van to the repair shop, to just relax and unwind.

Well then, let me quickly get to my bottom line: This short book is about eight discernible ways present-day Christians from Ohio to Ontario, New Mexico to New Brunswick, Arizona to Alberta, fail to be like their New Testament predecessors. It's about the negative effects these failures have on us. But mostly—*mostly*—this book is about antidotes for these flaws. It holds eight remedies that can add miracle dimensions to our present Christian living.

Yes, what I write about calls for changes. But I believe most people will agree, changes are necessary. Doing things in the church for the next five years in the same way they were done in the past five years won't move many tired Christians to where they need to be. Regele writes,

> The most important problem in the church today is a fundamental lack of clear, heart-grabbing vision. The church in America has no vision. It has programs and institutions and property and ministers and politically correct hymnals, but no vision.... We must do the work of revisioning the church for the twenty-first century—from the local congregation to the national denominational office. (*Death of the Church,* p. 229)

The Chapel Ministries, of which I have been director for the last two decades, has concentrated on developing tools that will help churches sharpen their vision of what Christ can do in their midst. Recapturing these important elements the church has lost will result in new life for individual believers and also for the whole body of Christ. So, if you are suddenly realizing that the troops, indeed, are tired, open yourself to the miracles of:

- ◆ Finding Tension's Good Side
- ◆ The 24/7 Church
- ◆ Christian Hospitality
- ◆ Pulpit/Pew Mutual Support
- ◆ Prayer with Fasting
- ◆ Telling Our Stories
- ◆ The Wider Kingship
- ◆ The Living Christ

These are untapped miracles for tapped-out Christians.

One last thought. When we eventually get a new van at the Chapel Ministries, I plan to have those same words painted on the side: "Dedicated to the vitality of the local church." That's because I dare to believe that both a vital faith and a vital church are still possible—even in North America! And though I'm now part of the graying demographic, I have always been a catalyst for change. That's not going to stop now. I believe the church can drastically affect its society. Infused with the very Spirit of Christ, we too can turn our world upside down.

CHAPTER ONE

UNTAPPED MIRACLE

FINDING TENSION'S GOOD SIDE

FLIP SIDE OF ADVERSITY

by Greg Asimakoupoulos

It's a coin toss
with a built-in loss.
At least that's how it seems.
Heads they win.
Tails I lose.
You know what I mean?
But how it seems
and how it is
aren't really both the same.
The flip side of adversity
is a gift that bears my name!

What wears you out?

It's surprising to me how different people are. Some friends require eight hours of sleep or at about 8:00 at night they start to fade. But that's just when others I know begin to come to life.

I've known work associates who were chronically tired because they had too much to do, and others whose energy levels were low because of boredom.

Watching television puts many to sleep. In church I've seen friends doze off while listening to a sermon. I thoroughly enjoyed a production of Shakespeare's *As You Like It*; but after act 1, scene 1, I noticed that two seats to my left someone apparently didn't find the play to be as *he* liked it. His tired eyes didn't open again until the applause sounded right before intermission.

Have you ever had a person conk out on you during a conversation? The other day I was driving an associate to a speaking engagement. I asked him a question, and when he didn't answer I rephrased it. Still no response. Then I looked over and saw that his chin had dropped onto his chest and he was gone to the world.

Are tensions hard on you? They tend to exhaust most men and women, especially those that take forever to get resolved. I'm referring to tensions such as:

◆ Staying competitive with people who are every bit your equal and more.
◆ Worrying about the resources, the connections, the opportunities being there for you at the right time to see your fondest dreams fulfilled.
◆ Having all—or even most—of the money you need.
◆ Figuring out if you should marry, and if so, finding the right mate.
◆ Getting beyond foolish mistakes and failures and sins that all too often mess up your life.
◆ Being afraid the world will pass you by because you couldn't keep up.
◆ Having the unexpected thwart your plans in some

cruel fashion—will you have an accident, get a disease, trust someone you shouldn't?

Facing too many tensions usually results in symptoms of fatigue. Over time, an abundance of problems can wear down even the strongest person.

TENSIONS AND TEAMS

When pressures mount, so does weariness. That happens in teachers and students, employers and employees, parishioners and pastors, those in their teens and twenties as well as folks in their sixties and seventies.

What's true of individuals also holds consistent for groups. Tensions can wear out entire teams of people. No one from Chicago questioned whether basketball's Dennis Rodman could rebound. What we wondered about was the toll the team would pay for all the ancillary problems he brought along with him, on court or off court. Even the Bull's coach, Phil Jackson, a master at player relationships, seemed a bit weary from time to time with the additional headaches brought on by Rodman's antics.

More than most church people realize, pastors spend a lot of time attempting to work amicably with difficult personality types. The idea of a church commissioner with the clout to suspend the problem players for inappropriate behavior might at first sound appealing. But I doubt that God's flock would give anyone 11-Sunday suspension powers (as the NBA Commissioner exercised in 1996 when he suspended Rodman for kicking a cameraman in the groin).

Fans can usually tell when a team is pooped. The players go through the motions, but their bursts of energy are short-lived. Before long, the signs of tiredness are obvious to all.

The same is true of churches. Lots of congregations are just plumb worn out. The members don't even fight all that much because it isn't worth the energy. Some time back they also gave up on any thoughts about being champions. That's a given. No one has to say it out loud; everybody knows it's true.

TIRED CHURCHES, TIRED CHRISTIANS

I wonder: Is your church a tired church?

A believer who's part of a fatigued church usually feels the same way in his or her personal relationship with Christ. The bloom is off the rose. Sure, such attenders know that Jesus is the Son of God, because there once was a special time when they individually experienced his miracle touch. But for whatever reason, at present they feel like they've pretty much exhausted what he's able to do. Now it's a matter of finishing out the life schedule with hopes that heaven proves better than their present suspicions indicate.

Are you a tapped-out Christian?

Living with a faith that's lost its fizz will prove a tension in itself. What you believe and have experienced spiritually is important, so you can't just casually let go of it. But you can't really embrace it either.

You can't embrace it because in many ways it appears not to be working. Christ hasn't proven himself as dramatic in answering your recent prayers the way he did your original request for forgiveness. These days the tensions, the struggles, the anxieties, the concerns you have strong feelings about—these don't appear to be priority items to him.

And guess what? You may be right!

Often our agenda is not his agenda. Our perspective is quite different from God's perspective. Our desires are often at odds with his desires. And if your faith is built on the premise of "What's in this for me?" then expectations that dead-end won't be all that infrequent. You could be part of a church filled with the very presence of God and still be exercising a feeble faith.

> **THE KEY: FATIGUE LIFTS WHEN GOD'S PEOPLE EXERCISE THE DISCIPLINE OF FINDING TENSION'S GOOD SIDE.**

THE FLIP SIDE OF TENSION

This book is about eight sensational ways for believers to get out of such spiritual cul-de-sacs. Here's the first one: *Fatigue lifts when God's people exercise the discipline of finding tension's good side.* By that I mean there's a reverse imprint on this spiritual coin. When the flip is made, you might need to stop calling tails again and again. Try heads for a change. Let me explain.

Looking back, I've found that some of the best things in my life didn't come about because of my careful planning. Instead, in the struggling that has often marked my walk of faith, God has allowed me to experience his unique direction in ways I never would have known, had I demanded that he do things according to my thinking.

Insisting on my own wishes has often resulted in spiritual delays and stoppages. By contrast, yielding to his strange yet wonderful ways has consistently ended up in exciting and productive faith adventures. Does that make sense?

I'm not asking whether the way God works his will in our lives always makes sense. Often it doesn't! Except in retrospect. But I'm wondering whether the attitude of faith I'm describing is understandable.

I inquire because I believe that finding tension's good side is a huge lesson more people need to learn. It's like the Joseph story being recycled for this generation. Joseph wouldn't have chosen to be thrown into a pit by his jealous older brothers. The humiliating situation of being falsely accused of making sexual advances toward Potiphar's wife was anything but welcomed. Then there was "The Strange Case of the Befriended Butler's Bad Memory." When released, this fellow prisoner totally forgot that Joseph had done him a colossal favor. But while others might have meant these events for evil, God's side of the coin read "Meant for good." Remember?

BIG TENSIONS ARE TOUGH TO HANDLE

Seeing tension's good side is also a Ruth-type narrative repeated for contemporary characters. She certainly didn't prefer being widowed early on. Gleaning the fields as an immigrant worker wasn't her priority choice. But these were divine givens that led to her eventually marrying Boaz and flipping all *his* coins! Then, low and behold, this Gentile woman, because of her faith, was also privileged to be included in the kingly line of both David and Christ.

In the midst of their tensions, neither Joseph nor Ruth could possibly have imagined what God had in mind. It's even less likely, had they known, that they could have pulled off his heavenly objectives on their own. Such an assignment would have taxed both of them well beyond their resources.

But they lived believing God was worth following. Even when it appeared he wasn't one whit concerned about their prayer requests, they kept looking for tension's flip side. My suspicion is that these people disciplined themselves to say, "I believe there's another option to this coin-calling that needs to be considered. Everything looks bad, but I'm choosing to affirm that the Lord is somehow working things out in his own inimitable way. Right now I can't see clearly what's happening, but my fatigue is sure to lift as I look each day for tension's good side."

A tired faith whines, "Why can't God see what's going on and give me a break?" A lively faith declares, "I choose to believe God is doing something wonderful, and in time he'll make everything clear."

I have a friend with tired faith. She knew God's hand on her life and ministered powerfully in days past. Then, through no fault of her own, she lost an important job. Now she wants a similar position or one a bit better. She'll be the judge of whether the next offer is as good as it should be. And she's been calling tails for some time now. She's been waiting for God to affirm *her* wishes for some time now. She's been tense about the situation for some time now. She's been angry for some time now. For some time now, she's been reluctant to look at the opposite side of the coin. She's still saying, "Do it my way, God." And she's slowly wearing down. Week by week she gets more and more depressed. Maybe someday she'll try calling heads. I hope so.

Hear me. I certainly appreciate what she's going through. It's probably every bit as hard as anything you or I have ever had to face. Her story hints of what Joseph or Ruth endured. These are pain-filled experiences. Big tensions are tough to handle.

FROM TENSION TO TESTIMONY

Speaking of big tensions, often such stories involve a number of people. For example, Acts 8 relates how practically the entire church in Jerusalem had persecution break out against it. Scripture reads that the believers were scattered. To be more precise, they left everything and fled for their lives. Many who risked staying in town were dragged from their homes and tossed into prison. That's not a pretty picture. Unfortunately, it's one that's being repeated in many countries today.

But the early church did what Christian brothers and sisters are doing even now in those tough settings. They lived believing that God is an expert at using all things, even the bad, for his good and ultimately for their good as well. So even in the incredibly tense times of persecution, they gave testimony to God's overarching goodness.

"Meanwhile, the believers who had fled from

Jerusalem during the persecution after Stephen's death traveled as far as Phoenicia, Cyprus, and Antioch of Syria. They preached the Good News, but only to Jews. However, some of the believers who went to Antioch from Cyprus and Cyrene began"—what? telling everyone about the awful persecution they had gone through? No, that wasn't it!—*"preaching to Gentiles about the Lord Jesus.* The power of the Lord was upon them, and large numbers of these Gentiles believed and turned to the Lord" (Acts 11:19-21, italics added).

Would the Jerusalem church have carried out such an ambitious missions program on its own? Probably not. I don't want to imply that God was responsible for the persecution. Nothing could be further from the truth—in New Testament times or in the present. I'm just noting that a live and vibrant faith asks, "How might God use this present tension to bring further glory to the name of Jesus?" And such a conviction assumes that in the process the Lord will be more than fair with his servants.

So, the early church had a choice. When they faced persecution, they could look at the negative and moan, "God, will we ever get our houses back? What about all the nice clothes we lost? Where were you when we pleaded and pleaded for help? What's your problem, Lord? Do you need a better hearing aid? Are you getting old or something?"

Or, as his servants, they could actively look for tension's good side—for how they could bring their Master even further benefit, all the while asking the Lord to hasten the time when they would be wise enough to understand what he was doing so they could serve him.

RX FOR TENSION RELIEF

This miracle mindset is not an easy one to acquire. It's a discipline that has to be exercised until it becomes habitual. To help with the process, let me recommend a simple prayer.

Caution: If I could, I'd make that word stand out like a flashing red light: CAUTION! CAUTION! CAUTION! *Don't race through what follows.*

I'm aware that people who are worn out by stress want immediate answers. And they're usually not too excited about changing how they react to their problems. But a change is almost always required.

If you went to a doctor and he said a certain medicine would help you, you would go to the trouble of making a trip to the pharmacy to get it. The prescription would probably cost more than you expected, not to mention the doctor's fee. But if you wanted relief, you'd do what you were told.

> I'M AWARE THAT PEOPLE WHO ARE WORN OUT BY STRESS WANT IMMEDIATE ANSWERS. BUT A CHANGE IS ALMOST ALWAYS REQUIRED.

As a minister with a solid reputation for helping people with their faith, I'm about to share an incredibly powerful prayer. But you need to *use* it! (If it makes you feel better, I'll charge you for it—okay, I won't. But don't minimize its effectiveness just because I'm offering it at no cost.) At the start, repeat the dosage at least two to three times a day. As the weeks progress, you'll most likely put the prayer into your own words. But don't stop using it until you feel that with the Lord's help you've begun to master what these tensions are doing to you, rather than remaining a slave to them.

The Tension's Good Side Prayer

Lord,
One of the untapped miracles in this book is to
see how you bring good out of our tensions.
Right now, a tension I'm facing personally is

_____.

I turn this situation over to you, knowing you
love me and are in control of my days.
Help me to live believing you are
constantly working in my behalf.
And let me be on the lookout today for
evidences of your miracle touch.
Amen

This prayer has a line that needs to be completed. Each time you use the prayer, you finish that open-ended sentence with whatever tension you're presently facing.

◆ Maybe it's a conflict with a colleague at work.
◆ It could be a pain in your side that's bothering you.
◆ Perhaps your car is stalling at unexpected times, but it's a hassle getting it to the garage, not to mention paying for what could be major repairs.

Here's a recent illustration from my own life. At the moment, a tension I'm facing personally is a lot of work to do with hardly enough time to get it all done. On top of that, our company is short-staffed. So once again, deadlines are hounding me.

From past struggles with workaholism, I know this is not a condition God approves of as a lifestyle. So my tails option is to say like I used to, "There's nothing I can do about this Lord. As the ministry grows, so does my workload. That's just the nature of things. You're lucky you have someone as committed as I am. But, to be truthful, it's hard to serve with a joyful spirit when it seems like the servant is committing more resources to these projects than the Master is!"

For me to call heads is to admit to the Lord, "I must be falling back into some old patterns. I've made a lot of progress with this sin, but I need to stay on my guard, don't I? I'll let today's tension be a reminder that you made me a human being, not a human doing."

Because I prayed the recommended prayer this morning, I turned down an early afternoon request to do a live 10:00 P.M. television interview. The Chicago station wanted me to come to the studio and respond to a fast-breaking news story. The program producer said he felt I was the perfect minister to offer a mature Christian response to what had happened. How's that for an enticing invitation? But to agree to do it would jam my schedule even worse. Having prayed this prayer earlier in the day slowed me down. Sure, this invitation was a great opportunity. But I chose to suggest someone who might do an even better job on the topic. Then, while the caller was still on the line, I prayed a short prayer asking God to help him quickly find who was exactly right for the interview.

Will that station ever call me again? I don't know. But

as I went back to my more immediate responsibilities, I had a sense of God whispering to my heart, "Not bad, David. For an old dog, you're still capable of learning new tricks. Good for you!" This wasn't what I would call a bona fide miracle. But it felt good because I didn't let something add to my pressures like I've done so often in the past. (My grown kids often remind me that one of the most repeated lines they heard from me at the height of my workaholic years was, "I'm so tired I can't see straight!" Believe me, I know about being tapped out.)

Incidentally, with the line in the prayer that reads, "Let me be on the lookout today for evidences of your miracle touch," don't forget to emphasize the words *be on the lookout*. Otherwise you might think of miracles as ordinary occurrences. Obviously, if they were commonplace, they wouldn't be miracles! It generally takes a while before you can see what God is doing behind the scenes. I remind you again of Joseph and Ruth. These stories took years to unfold. You do have to maintain a stance of being actively on the lookout. And you must hold to a conviction that miracles aren't really all that difficult for God. In fact, he seems to enjoy pulling them off at just the right time, especially in response to our requests.

It's important to know that this remarkable prayer I've given you works marvelously for churches as well as for individuals. What kind of tensions do churches struggle with? What about issues like:

◆ A neighborhood starting to change?
◆ The denomination ordaining homosexuals?
◆ A pastor being forced to resign?

◆ Catholics or Baptists or whatever group starting a building program on the adjoining property?

◆ People arguing about the use of drama on Sunday morning?

◆ The budget being underfunded for the third year straight?

◆ The dilemma of a congregation that is obviously aging?

◆ A youth pastor having been sexually involved with several church teens?

◆ Irresolvable differences regarding the role of women?

◆ A sizeable contingency threatening to pull out of the church?

The list goes on and on. That's because there are all kinds of tensions that push church people to the point of exhaustion.

So fill in the blank. Right now, a tension we're facing as a church is:

_____

_____

Then, instead of insisting that God answer your requests for the church in the exact way you think he should, start looking for creative ways he might use what is happening to bring glory to himself. Stop thinking about what's going on merely from your perspective. Attempt to align your thoughts with what you sense God is doing. After all, "We know that in all things God works for the good of those who love him, who have been called according to his purpose" (Romans 8:28).

TENSIONS OF TIME AND TIDE

Years ago, my grandfather Jess came to Illinois from Nova Scotia. As a boy, I remember listening to stories he told about the Bay of Funday, which boasts the highest and lowest tides in all the world. When the water was out, Grandpa Ben said it left mud flats that stretched for miles. The old fishermen drove stakes in the ground, tied lines to them, and baited the hooks. When the water came in, the fish would feed on these lures and practically catch themselves. Then they would be stranded on the land when the tide receded.

One time, Grandpa said, Old Man Shaw had taken longer than he expected with other jobs, so he got a late start checking his lines. This one had a fish, the next one didn't. Two more with nothing, then another catch.

"Oh, one thing I need to remind you of, David," said my grandfather. "The fog in that area could roll in like a blanket. And while Old Shaw was out on this mudbank, that's what happened to him. It was thicker than a boy like you can imagine. And the combination of a late start, the fog, and his awareness that the tide would soon be fast coming in combined to put this old-timer in a precarious position. If he just forgot about his last couple lines, he could beat it back to higher ground. But Old Man Shaw was greedy."

Now the storytelling got more intense. "The old codger was down on his hands and knees feeling for the stakes in the fog. He found one. He quickly pulled in the line, which had a good-sized fish on it. Only one or two more to check, then he'd better head back. But he couldn't find the next post—and while groping for it, he got turned around, confused in his sense of direction."

Now, little boy that I was, I sat up straight on my chair, totally engrossed in the story and wondering whether or not Old Man Shaw was going to make it. Talk about *big tension!*

"Young David," said Grandpa, "you can still crawl and it doesn't wear you out. But for an old man like Shaw with a couple of good-sized fish on his back, it tired him. That's why he was huffing and puffing. Now he forgot about those lost lines and concentrated on his safety. He began to run—careful, though, not to stumble over a stake. He thought he should have been to higher ground; he'd been going long enough to reach it. Maybe if he changed directions slightly. His heart raced, because running in fog isn't just hard work, it's terrifying. He even tossed his precious fish aside. They didn't mean anything if this was a matter of life or death. And it was. You know why?"

> I SAT UP STRAIGHT ON MY CHAIR, WONDERING WHETHER OR NOT OLD MAN SHAW WAS GOING TO MAKE IT. TALK ABOUT BIG TENSION!

"Because he was lost, Grandpa?" I responded breathlessly.

"Well, yes, of course he was lost. And the fog confused him. But more than that, now he could feel water on his feet. The tide was coming in and Shaw knew it would come in fast."

"Did he die?"

"He probably would have—if he hadn't tried something different."

"What did he do?"

"Well, he did something he wasn't used to doing. Suddenly he yelled, 'GOD, HELP ME!' Then he stopped running and just stood there—and he thought he saw a light. Off in the distance and up away, he thought he saw this glow.

"'Maybe that's the light on the steeple of the church up the hill,' he said to himself. And he started stumbling in that direction. 'God, I hope it's you. God, I hope it's you,' he repeated. Then he blurted out, 'God, if you get me out of this mess, I'll start going to that church. Every Sunday I'll go. And I'll live like they tell me, and I'll never be greedy again, and—and I won't cuss.' And Old Man Shaw vowed to stop every bad thing he could think of as he kept half walking and half stumbling toward that light, which was now getting more and more clear, because (would you believe?) the fog was lifting. That was a miracle, wasn't it, David? And sure enough, he finally made it back safe."

"And did he do what he said, Grandpa?"

"Well, the people in town were amazed. They tell me he was one changed man. It's pretty remarkable what God will do to bring a stubborn old fellow to himself."

"I like that story, Grandpa."

"Grandpa Ben likes you, young Mister David."

The fog lifted when Old Man Shaw finally gave up on tails and decided in his panic to try heads.

If tensions have worn you down, and tails hasn't been doing well for you, I've spelled out what your other option is. Want to call heads for a change?

Here's how. Write the prayer I prescribed on several three-by-five cards. Always have it available to use again and again and again and again—at least until you're off the dangerous flats and safe on shore. Because you see, fatigue —like a fog—lifts when God's people exercise the discipline of finding tension's good side.

CHAPTER TWO

UNTAPPED MIRACLE 2

THE 24/7 CHURCH

BEYOND PRIMETIME

by Greg Asimakoupoulos

Your vision for my life, Lord,
is more than 20/20;
it's 24/7.
To be your person everyday,
that is what I seek.
60 Minutes a week
is not enough to focus my eyes on you.
It may be Primetime,
but it's not the only time
you're at work around me.
You're on the job with me.
You're in the car beside me.
Your Spirit's flowing through me
in everything I do.
And when I have an inner hunch
to ask a friend to go for lunch,
I know that as we sip our soup
my words will come from you.

It's exhausting trying to live with two different core iden-
tities. The gay community has certainly attempted to

make this point as it forces the nation to come to grips with its agenda. Not too long ago, Ellen Degeneres, the television comedienne, evoked controversy by "coming out of the closet" when she declared herself homosexual right along with the character she plays in her sitcom. Despite my personal sadness regarding this lifestyle, I'm aware of the acute mental strain such individuals must endure as they attempt to be one thing in certain settings and an almost totally different person somewhere else.

"For me," the actress stated in an interview with *Time* (April 14, 1997), "this has been the most freeing experience . . . I don't have to worry about somebody saying something about me, or a reporter trying to find out information. Literally, as soon as I made this decision, I lost weight. My skin has cleared up. I don't have anything to be scared of, which I think outweighs whatever else happens in my career."

This intense struggle to somehow live within the truth—even if it's a truth many people strongly disapprove of, which could jettison a career—gives a sense of the fearsome toll it takes to live a life of duplicity. Those who "come out of the closet" speak of experiencing a tremendous sense of relief. This is the case despite the fact the fallout from such a declaration is often enormously negative.

Again, while not in any way endorsing homosexuality as a lifestyle, I can at least feel sorry for those who attempt to cope with the day-to-day strain of living out a lie—behaving one way in one setting and another somewhere else.

DOUBLE-MINDED CHRISTIANS

You probably know people who are living in duplicity—not in the gay community, but in the church community. I'm referring to Christians who appear to be one thing on Sunday morning and something quite different during the week. To observe someone like this is almost like watching two distinct personalities. You know at least part of them is being untrue to the beliefs and convictions held in the heart. And aside from whether it's right or wrong, this kind of duplicity places people under intense strain because maintaining such a double-minded lifestyle is exhausting.

> **THE KEY:** THE INABILITY TO INTEGRATE ONE'S SUNDAY IDENTITY WITH MONDAY THROUGH SATURDAY CAUSES CHRISTIANS TO QUIT TRYING ALTOGETHER.

Maybe that's why so many in our ranks are tired all the time! Don't misunderstand me. My concern isn't with intentional and unmistakable hypocrites. From my observation of North American churchgoers, these are actually quite rare. Instead, I'm thinking about the large number of Christians who worship regularly on weekends and are often considered the core of the church. You know. People like us.

Let's imagine that this past weekend an objective news reporter visited the church you or I attend. The assignment: To observe what goes on when the church is gathered, then to investigate the visible impact this has on people's behavior when the congregation scatters. Assuming this reporter is competent and fair, what might such investigative journalism reveal?

Let me illustrate with an observation this reporter might have made at my church. Most congregations enjoy hymns and choruses, so you'll probably relate. Last Sunday our people sang this verse of "Oh Jesus, I Have Promised":

O, let me feel Thee near me; the world is ever near,
I see the sights that dazzle, the tempting sounds
   I hear,
My foes are ever near me, around me and within;
But Jesus, draw thou nearer, and shield my soul
   from sin.

Following the congregation throughout the week, would this reporter find that singing such hymns is just a church tradition, with most people paying little attention to the words? Or would it be the opposite? Might many remember they pleaded in song for Jesus to be nearer than the world, and because of this, they choose to turn off *Melrose Place,* Howard Stern's radio show, or the Home Shopping Channel? That's the reporter's question: Will church people make any connection between the words they sing about "tempting sounds" or "sights that dazzle" and the tangible events in daily life? Or will they be seen living double lives?

Our pastor's sermon last Sunday included a strong appeal to consistently make wise choices. We were told that by our choices we can make our world darker or we can spread God's light. It was a clear and forceful presentation to which I could say, "Amen."

But what if that reporter made some on-site visits to others in the congregation, like the junior high student who sat in the pew across from me? Did she choose to be honest, even when she saw others in her Spanish class cheating on Monday's vocabulary quiz? Or the man behind me in his mid-forties who struggles with depression. By Tuesday afternoon, will he still remember what he heard at church and choose to carefully guard against the dark thoughts he too often allows to inhabit his mind?

I suspect the answers to those questions would also be indicative of something else. My belief is that where a strong connection is found between what happens on Sunday and who people are the rest of the week, we'll also see great vitality within the congregation. And the less the two worlds relate, the more we will see indications of spiritual fatigue among the troops. That's because *the inability to integrate one's Sunday identity with Monday through Saturday eventually causes Christians to quit trying or to stop caring altogether.*

THE CHURCH SCATTERED

I'm a minister. Most of those in my profession don't identify all that closely with this problem. Do you know why? It's because the world of the clergy is more integrated than that of the average church-goer. A minister is paid and expected to live in a churchly fashion all week long. Because of a collar, which is a reminder every time it's snapped on, an ever-present Bible in the briefcase, or a library filled with books on spiritual life and theology, or a *Reverend* or *Pastor* in front of our names, we're regularly brought back to the reality of who we are and what we are supposed to be.

That's not true for most parishioners. The bottom line for them in weekend services is seldom the same standard with which they're evaluated the rest of the week. That's why it's so important for church leaders to make the connection between troops that are tired and pulpit challenges that fail to adequately relate to the everyday worlds of those who listen to us. That's an issue we'll address in greater depth in chapter 4, "Untapped Miracle #4: Pulpit/Pew Mutual Support." Right now, I'll just state that while I'm pleased about the work that's been done in recent years to improve what takes place when the church is *gathered,* the great power of the church won't be released until large numbers of our people are taught how to be the church *scattered.*

It's going to take a major effort to resolve this energy-zapping dichotomy. So much happens in people's lives today, church services by themselves don't have the same impact they did several decades back. The truth is, people today can go to a good movie and come out feeling profoundly moved. But two days later almost everyone will have pretty much forgotten what they saw. Why? Because for the majority of us, life moves at too fast a clip to remember what touched us a day or two before. And the entertainment industry deals with budgets of tens and even hundreds of millions of dollars per film! How can the church compete in providing a lasting "punch" when even the highly funded competition is often ineffective?

I believe that in day-to-day practice many church

people have become "secular Christians." For whatever reason, we've restricted our thinking about where we are spiritually to the parameters of our worship services. Yes, we oppose secularism. We think it's bad. We fight it in name. But in actuality, we've pretty much succumbed to it.

According to the dictionary, *secularism* is the belief that religion shouldn't enter into mainstream society, such as the worlds of government or education. The term *secular television* implies a media system that gives only restricted exposure to religious thinking. A secular magazine like *Time* won't really allow for a spiritual interpretation of the news. When it comes to secular thinking, religion is seen pretty much as what occurs in churches during the regular service. Beyond that, it's not viewed as a major player in the events that unfold.

THE 24/7 LIFE

If I'm right, if the dynamics of everyday faith have been lost, if we fill the air with praises to Jesus on Sunday and hardly have time to think about him the other six days, if that kind of duplicity is more who we are than we care to admit, then it's no wonder our faith isn't all that alive. We're squandering energy attempting to juggle two different lifestyles. To experience an incredible new energy source, it's time for the Christian believer to be one person, not two, and to start experiencing how empowering that singularity of living can be.

In the church we need to talk more about how the faith relates to the home, the workplace, and the community. We need to rethink how people's spiritual gifts function Monday through Saturday. We must come up with more illustrations of Christians demonstrating their faith in buildings and on grounds other than those owned by the church. But most importantly, as believers we have to stop defaulting on the other 100-plus waking hours we have outside of Sunday morning.

The second miracle of eight I want you to begin thinking about is the 24/7 church—a body of believers that influences their world 24 hours a day, 7 days a week. It's much like the faith that characterized the early church of the New Testament.

I got that comparison in early because I can almost hear someone moaning: "Twenty-four/seven! That smacks of Las Vegas or Reno, open every day of the week, any hour of the day, where you can gamble non-stop. The picture I have is of some middle-aged smoker sitting on a stool, repeatedly pulling down the lever on a slot machine. Her eyes are glazed over and she's so out of it she's hardly aware of what's happening. That 24/7 phrase may sound exhilarating to you, but not to me!"

Well then, let me paint a different word picture for you. I want to make it as attractive as I can, because I believe a 24/7 church is absolutely imperative in re-energizing our tired troops. Far too many Christians have a problem with living double lives, and it's going to take a concerted effort for us to learn to live like the man I want to refer to next.

"OUT OF THE CLOSET" FAITH

When the Medes conquered the Babylonians, the reigning monarch, Darius, was about 62 years old. Being about that age myself, I can see why he appointed three capable administrators, with 120 satraps answering to them. One of the three was so obviously distinguished that the king planned to appoint him as his COO—his Chief Operating Officer. The others, getting wind of what was about to happen, opposed the idea. They tried to find evidence of corruption in the way this man ran his office, but they couldn't. Eventually, they came to the conclusion that their attack would have to be on spiritual grounds.

You see, Daniel was a 24/7 Hebrew believer living out his faith in exile. He had been raised in Jerusalem, but years earlier that city had fallen to mighty Babylon. Now the Medes had defeated them. Through it all, Daniel just kept living for God. Even as a key leader in another country's government, he was assertively, intentionally "out of the closet" regarding his faith.

He openly lived his faith every hour of every day. When you read his story in Scripture, it's almost like you've finished two or three biographies. He outlived kings and emperors. Even in the Book of Daniel, chapter 6, after decades of living a life of singular faith, we find an account, not of an old-timer showing signs of wearing down, but of a man still full of 24/7 spiritual vitality.

You'll recall how Daniel's opponents tried to confine his faith, to keep it within certain bounds. For 30 days no prayers were to be said, except to the king; that was the new scandalous law. The result was the incredible account of Daniel in the lion's den. This incident was perhaps the highlight of Daniel's days, but it's also characteristic of all the heroic episodes of his past. And this is a man noted for his resourcefulness, his health, and his accomplishments. You might even say his single-minded faith in God was his source of energy.

To discover exactly how miraculously energizing it can be to live as a 24/7 believer, we need to learn to be the same people every hour of every day, like Daniel. If living decidedly Christian means jettisoning a career, so be it. Hopefully, it won't come to that. But regardless, we need to be God's man or woman in spite of external threats. This is an incredibly powerful characteristic the church needs to rediscover.

> WE NEED TO BE THE SAME PEOPLE EVERY HOUR OF EVERY DAY. THIS IS AN INCREDIBLY POWERFUL CHARACTERISTIC.

Daniel's habit was to pray in his upstairs room with his windows open toward Jerusalem. I suppose for 30 days he could have shut the windows, but he chose to do otherwise. By not being secretive, of course, he made himself vulnerable.

Today the simple matter of whether or not to pray in public before a meal may be what determines how open God's people are about their faith. It's not easy for a new Christian to pray before a meal in the factory lunchroom. Even bowing your head for silent prayer in the school cafeteria can be a defining moment for a Christian high-school or college student.

Every now and then, our son Joel, who has produced our daily television show, is called to work on the NBC crew for special sporting events. During the 1997 National Basketball Association playoffs, he was tagged to work for the Bulls' home games at the United Center. Sitting on the players' bench beside Michael Jordan, filming the pre-game and post-game interviews, and going into the champions' locker room is a big deal in a city that idolizes the members of its winning teams. However, working with TV crew members who are on the road for months, who are jaded about the whole sports celebrity business, and whose language is profane beyond belief, is a challenge for any Christian serious about living a daily life of faith and commitment to Christ. While debriefing the winning championship game with those of us eager to hear his "inside" tales, Joel mentioned the cynicism of the television professionals, but then he talked about bowing his head to pray quietly at a meal. He was suddenly aware of a deafening silence from those sitting around him. And he was also keenly aware that the language of his coworkers improved a bit after lunch!

TO, THROUGH, AND TALK ABOUT

It takes courage, determination, and practice to be decidedly Christian in these kinds of settings. So let's start with something easier. An old saying goes, "What's learned with pleasure is learned full measure." That's why I'd like to get you into the 24/7 mindset through a kind of game format. The name of the game is To, Through, and Talk About.

Here's rule number one: Look for ways God speaks *to* you in settings other than Sunday mornings in church. It could be through Scripture, an answer to prayer, a helpful comment someone makes, a thought from a book you're reading, a Christian radio program you hear, a memory, a song, a letter, a circumstance, a kind deed in your behalf, a phone call, a gift of money, or any other way you recognize God's touch in your life outside of the normal church context. Each day, Monday through Saturday, write down one time God speaks to you in a special manner.

Rule number two: Look for ways God ministers *through* you during the week. Once again, this can happen in a nearly unlimited number of ways. You listen to somebody's troubles. You help a person financially. You spend serious time in prayer for a friend. You prepare a meal for someone in need. You call an acquaintance who is lonely. You go out of your way to be friendly to a grump. You show God's love to a child. You care for a neighbor. You show patience with a coworker. You stay late without complaining to finish up an important job. You talk to someone about Jesus. The question you must answer is, *How did Christ minister through me to someone else?* Keep track of that on a daily basis as well—to and through.

What's happening is that you're getting used to thinking about your faith 24/7. By watching for ways God is speaking to you, you're acknowledging the reality of his presence in your life outside of church. If he can speak to you at home or work or school, you're saying he must be there with you. As you look for tangible evidence of his presence in your Monday through Saturday life, you'll also be made more constantly aware of that truth. That's going to help you with any double thinking you're struggling to eliminate.

In the same way, God can't speak through you to someone else unless he's there with you. You can't look for opportunities to allow God to speak through you if you've left him in the sanctuary on Sunday morning. That's why this second part of the game is also a great way to eliminate duplicity in your day-to-day life. It's hard to be double-minded when you're looking for ways to share God's words and actions with others.

Now, here's rule number three, and you'll have everything you need to play the To, Through, and Talk About game: Talk to someone else about what you're observing. Get used to discussing with others how your faith is spilling out of Sunday into Monday through Saturday—how you delight in being the church gathered, but also how the church works when scattered.

To, through, and talk about. Got it?

At first I was hesitant to suggest a simple game like this because I wasn't certain how seriously you'd take it. But I was equally reluctant to call for a response that might prove too daring because I don't want to scare anyone off. The lion's den may have been the location of Daniel's greatest victory, but it's still a place most of God's people would prefer to stay out of—for a while, anyway.

So let's back up a bit. Let's take another run at things. Are you someone who has trouble being as enthusiastic about your faith on Monday through Saturday as you were on Sunday morning? Would the people with whom you regularly rub shoulders during the week be surprised to see you make choices based on the beliefs you affirm on the Lord's Day? Might they, in fact, be surprised to learn you attended church every weekend? Are you among the tired troops whose double-identity problems keep you from being energized about your faith? Do you need some kind of miracle to see this problem resolved?

Well then, wouldn't looking for how God speaks to you each day be a helpful exercise? Wouldn't filing these discoveries in your head be a good method of keeping track of what God's doing, and wouldn't writing them down somewhere be even more beneficial? And what about making notes on how God speaks through you? Should you actually go to the effort of writing down both the to's and throughs? Can you come up with a better way of starting to get used to the 24/7 aspect of your faith? Who can you begin talking with about your discoveries? If you carry through on this assignment, can you see it energizing your faith? Will this game help you from falling into the secular/Christian trap? If everyone in your church got into the To, Through, and Talk About game, wouldn't the entire congregation benefit?

Thinking through your answers to those questions, are you willing to make a commitment to begin playing this game today?

What if I had suggested that everyone carry a Bible to work? Would that have been a better idea? Lots of people bring their Bibles to church. Maybe taking them to school or the factory or the office or the store would be a faster way to instill the 24/7 concept in people's minds.

No, I still prefer the To, Through, and Talk About approach. A Bible can all too easily be shoved into a drawer or hidden on a shelf. We can carry it but not attend to it. This spiritual game forces the integration of head-truth into everyday circumstances. Once you've begun to play, I'm certain you will understand why I find it so beneficial.

Now, perhaps you're someone who is still feeling a strong sense of resistance to this idea of being a 24/7 Christian. You may be thinking, "I can hardly get through a church day without making an un-Christlike comment or letting somebody know I'm angry. I'm nowhere near acting out my faith at school or on the job!" If that's the situation you're facing, then the spiritual tiredness you're feeling must be overwhelming.

This week when you're among God's people, focus on being truthful about yourself and your struggles. Ask God to give you an opportunity to talk to someone else about the area of sin or temptation you're trying so hard to cover up. Chances are good that your honesty will actually be a gift to those around you, allowing them to open up and be vulnerable, too. And God can speak to you, through someone else, much more easily if your fellow believers know what you're going through. Give it a try. It's an important first step in experiencing the miracle energizer of becoming a 24/7 Christian.

REAL-LIFE EXAMPLES

Let me see if I can explain some practical ways this 24/7 experience can have an impact on others.

A friend I pray with has a daughter who has been in and out of the church for some years. As an adult, she's fallen away from attending regularly. She works as a beautician and does a good job for her clients. A while ago, she decided to change her place of employment. She was having trouble with her boss and heard of a new award-winning salon. Now, it happened that the manager there was a Christian. This gave her a little pause, but she decided to make the change.

It was only a few days after taking the job that she discovered she was pregnant with her second child. She worried how her new employer would respond. She knew what her former boss would have said, disgruntled at having to give her time off just after her training was complete. Nervous about bringing up the topic, she stalled, waiting for the most advantageous moment.

Late one afternoon, after she had finished with all her clients, she felt a little sick to her stomach and asked to go home early. The next day the Christian salon-owner inquired whether she was pregnant. Reluctantly admitting this was so, she explained that she hadn't known about it until after the job change. "Oh, that's great news!" was his joyful response. "I think your little girl needs a new brother or sister."

My friend's daughter was deeply touched by this show of kindness and this affirmation of the new life she was carrying. Here was a shop owner who was living out his faith 7 days a week, 24 hours a day. Even though this young mother wasn't in church very often, she was still seeing the love of Jesus in her employer's life. That's the extra bonus that comes from being a 24/7 Christian.

I regularly have breakfast with a doctor who has become a new Christian. He talks with great delight about how he now sees his office as a place of ministry. He prays for his patients and tries to treat them with the gentle touch of Jesus.

My hope is that he will not be like another couple who were deeply involved in the school board and in various civic activities before they became Christians. Embracing their new faith, they chose to drop these involvements to spend more time in church ministries. Unfortunately, they saw "ministry" as being limited to activities *within* the local church. Over a period of years, they not only lost all their secular contacts, but they became like so many who find all their hours occupied with the organization and the "in" group. I'm hoping that this won't happen with my doctor friend.

EVEN THOUGH THIS YOUNG MOTHER WASN'T IN CHURCH VERY OFTEN, SHE WAS STILL SEEING THE LOVE OF JESUS IN HER EMPLOYER'S LIFE.

In our churches, we need to spotlight the stories of what people are doing during the week as they live out their faith. We should be encouraging people to use their gifts in settings outside the church building. We must help them see how hospitals and grocery stores and repair shops and schools and construction sites are potential places for ministry. And as we hear about the impact these 24/7 Christians are having, others within the church will be encouraged and energized as well.

24/7 EVANGELISM

Acting as a 24/7 Christian is also one of the best ways you can attract others to life-changing faith in Jesus

Christ. Whether you want to admit it or not, duplicity shows. And whether or not you're aware of it, your single-minded Christian lifestyle will have a profound influence on others.

The pastor of a nearby church related the story of a young woman named Debbie who came to Christ through the consistent, 24/7 actions of a young couple in the congregation. Debbie had become acquainted with several members of the church when she became pregnant out of wedlock. She had decided to give the baby up for adoption, and they provided needed physical and emotional support throughout the process.

She became especially friendly with a woman named Carol, who was just a few years older than Debbie. Carol was engaged to a young man from the church named David. This young couple kept in close touch long after Debbie's pregnancy was over, eventually leading her to faith in Christ.

It wasn't until years later that Debbie told Carol this story: "When you and David were dating, I wanted to see if your faith was for real. You probably think I decided to become a Christian because you prayed for me and because you showed Christ's love to me during a difficult time. That was a part of it, but it's not the biggest reason. Before you got married, when we'd all get together, I'd always try to leave your apartment first. Then I'd sit outside in my car to see if David would go home or if he'd spend the night. I just couldn't believe it, but every single time, within 15 or 20 minutes I'd see David kiss you goodnight and leave. You guys really were practicing what you believed, even when you thought nobody was watching."

The 24/7 lifestyle of this young couple not only benefited them, it influenced the eternal future of a young woman seeking genuine faith. In turn, her conversion to Christianity touched and spiritually energized the entire congregation. And most all, I'm convinced it pleased the Lord himself.

As you read through the gospels it's extremely clear that Christ had little tolerance for religious hypocrites. To his disciples he declared, "If anyone would come after me, he must deny himself and take up his cross daily and follow me" (Luke 9:23, NIV). He didn't ask for those willing to follow him

> "YOU GUYS REALLY WERE PRACTICING WHAT YOU BELIEVED, EVEN WHEN YOU THOUGHT NOBODY WAS WATCHING."

on the Sabbath, but for those who would take up his cross daily. And this call is as impacting for us in the church today as it was for Christ's first disciples.

Let me go back to where I began this chapter. The gay community isn't really all that large. Most researchers say that homosexuals make up only about three or four percent of the total population. Yet they are highly committed people—willing to take a stand— and consequently, they exercise considerable influence.

The Christian church population is easily ten times larger. But most agree that in many ways our influence is on the wane. A big reason for this is that we have allowed our faith to be confined to what happens in the church building. I say we desperately need to break out of those confines. And we have much better reasons than those who "come out of the closet" to avow a homosexual lifestyle.

Yes, I'm convinced an incredible miracle will unfold in your life as you begin practicing a 24/7 Christian lifestyle. You'll begin to see God at work in your day-to-day life, not just on Sunday morning. You'll experience incredible new energy as you eliminate the duplicity that "taps out" so many of God's followers. But even more, you'll energize those around you—people both inside and outside the church.

CHAPTER THREE

UNTAPPED MIRACLE 3

CHRISTIAN HOSPITALITY

A LITURGY OF LOVE

by Greg Asimakoupoulos

We pass the peace in worship.
We pass the time at home.
And when we pass it with others,
the latter helps the former
make more sense.

So pass the food
and chew the fat
and brew a cup of care,
and you will share a peace
you never knew possible.

Some call it hospitality.
For me, it's a liturgy of love,
a ritual of grace,
a means by which my simple home
becomes a hallowed place.

Sometimes nighttime television host David Letterman's
"Top Ten" lists are clever, but I still don't often watch

him. My reason is that I find his approach to conversation entirely superficial. His show may be a good vehicle in displaying how witty he is, but I find little substance in what's covered.

When actress Farah Fawcett was his guest, a furor arose over whether or not she was on drugs or just acting like it. Apparently her manner of speaking was shallow and disjointed. But Letterman commented that he didn't notice anything unusual and that Ms. Fawcett was always a welcome guest. It appears she fits the pattern for a Letterman conversation partner.

Is competitor Jay Leno any better in the way he relates to people? Hardly! In my opinion, neither of these men model traits of a mature conversationalist.

Accusing someone of being superficial is hardly a compliment. It means that his or her conversations remain on the surface, lacking in any real depth. In my opinion, superficial talk does little more than put people to sleep. That's probably a good quality for a late-night television talk-show host, since most viewers are on the way to bed, but it's not a great way to build stimulating, meaningful relationships. The small talk, the word plays, the name dropping, the self-centered anecdotes repeated time and again—all leave me asking, "Isn't there more to life than this?"

SMALL TALK

How many times has a wife complained that her husband is a grunting couch potato once he gets home from work? And what husband appreciates a spouse who fails to grow and improve herself, winding up only able to converse on the level of her children? Either of these problems can quickly drain the creative energy from a marriage.

Locations where superficial conversations often take place include school buses, commuter train stations, office coffee break gatherings—and unfortunately, church lobbies before and after worship services.

"Hi, good to see you again. Doing well?"

"Not bad. And you?"

"Okay, except for this hot weather."

"Yeah, thank heavens for air conditioning."

"That's for sure. Take it easy."

"You too."

Interesting? Caring? Stimulating? No way! But sadly typical. So am I saying that Christians are basically superficial? Is shallowness the result of spending hours in the company of Jesus?

GOING DEEPER

Actually, Christ himself brought incredible energy to his conversations and relationships. Even worldly people enjoyed being around Jesus when he walked the earth. Is that because our Lord was a wise-cracking David Letterman or Jay Leno type?

The accounts of Jesus in the Scriptures obviously deny this assessment. Then why would church people be content to allow superficial conversations to characterize them? Don't we realize that small talk wears thin, leaving us depleted rather than renewed?

Well, I don't believe we Christians should resign ourselves to being stunted conversationalists because of the quality of our in-church conversations. Mostly, we've allowed circumstances to limit us.

First of all, the few minutes before or after a worship service are hardly adequate for in-depth conversation. Add to this limiting time factor the lack of privacy due to crowded spaces, and it's a wonder some people are as skilled as they are at discovering how friends are really doing. I mean, how empathetic can you be to someone who says she just lost her job when there's only a minute and a half before you're late picking up your one-year-old from the nursery?

People in the New Testament church didn't have multiple services with parking lots needing to be emptied and re-parked in precision efficiency. They didn't have one family member in Christian ed class, another serving as an usher, and a third rushing downstairs for a quick meeting of the Property Committee. And they didn't have to say, "Easter dinner's at Grandma's house a hundred miles away and we're due at 1:00 and it's already 11:15 (quick gasp for air)—so let's catch up next week, okay?" People of the early church regularly shared meals in homes, which allowed more than adequate time to find out what was going on in one another's lives.

EVERYBODY'S WELCOME

With this in mind, my wife and I decided to make hospitality the key gift we would maximize as we recently began attending a new church. Some readers might not consider hospitality a legitimate gift of the Holy Spirit, but we do. The apostle Peter mentions it specifically in his epistle: "Offer hospitality to one another without grumbling. Each one should use whatever gift he has received to serve others, faithfully administering God's grace in its various forms" (1 Peter 4:9–10, NIV).

This church has a new minister and not a very large congregation. It would be difficult to seat many more than 100 in the sanctuary. But space didn't present a problem in the 8:00 A.M. service, because only about 20 people were attending anyway.

You might think with that few it would be easy to get beyond superficialities on a Sunday morning. But getting acquainted is still hard. During the traditional passing of the Peace people would say, "Welcome" and "It's good to see you again," but that's about as far as it went. After you've hugged everyone and made a gracious comment or two, the allotted time is gone.

> **DURING THE TRADITIONAL PASSING OF THE PEACE, PEOPLE WOULD SAY, "IT'S GOOD TO SEE YOU," BUT THAT'S ABOUT AS FAR AS IT WENT.**

So we decided to start having people over for brunch following the service. We can seat nine around the dining room table and a second table is available if necessary. Our plan was to conduct hands-on training in how to open homes so that as the congregation grows, there will be the option of several places people can go following the early service.

Homes are warm settings. And a Sunday brunch doesn't need to rival what's available at the local Holiday Inn's all-you-can-eat buffet to be enjoyable. In fact, we've found it's not a bad idea to have people bring different menu items—a coffee cake, fruit, bagels, juice, whatever.

Not everyone comes every week, and most Sundays someone new joins us. Since it's an "everybody's welcome" invitation, we never have a head count in advance. But extra place settings are ready, or we just remove what's not needed. We strive for an informal, relaxed setting, so adjustments aren't all that much trouble.

Now, just because people are fed and relaxed doesn't mean they will automatically open up to one another. Even with plenty of time to talk, it's entirely possible to fill it with superficial chitchat. That's why we see our job as hosts to steer the conversation into meaningful directions. This is best done by asking the right kinds of questions.

THOUGHT-PROVOKING QUESTIONS

It's interesting how the way a question is asked can make it easier for people to share frankly about who they are and where they're coming from. "What do you do for a living?" will get one kind of response. "Tell me what's good and what's bad about your job" is probably a better question. If you want to learn about the inside of a person, you have to go beyond finding out the tasks he or she performs.

"What's a good memory you have related to church?" usually prompts positive replies from people. "Tell us about someone who influenced your life in a good way, and who plays that role for you now?" is another good question.

I don't assume all the people who come for brunch are believers. A foreign student with a different religious background came to the church and responded to our weekly invitation. Some good questions for this kind of visitor might be: "If you had the opportunity to travel anywhere you wanted, where would you go, and why?" or "What's a movie you really enjoyed, and why did you like it so much?" or "If you had an opportunity to relive a day in your life, which one would you pick, and why?" Sometimes we might be more up front, asking, "What observations about Christianity are you making during your stay here?" Good questions get beyond yes and no answers. And I have found that a group of people can become quite skilled in asking one another thought-provoking questions.

Recently, a visitor who works at a museum came to both church and brunch. Her area of expertise was snails. While I was desperately trying to think of what in the world I could ask on that topic, a member of the group said effusively, "Oh, what a wonderful subject! I've always wanted to know more about snails. Tell me about one kind that's especially interesting to you." Would you believe, the group was soon caught up in a 20-minute conversation that was absolutely fascinating!

It's important not only to ask good questions, but to listen to people's responses. Quite often I hear them say things around the table like, "I'm going through a divorce that's very painful," or "I've been without work for over two months now," or "My son was picked up by the police again last week." When something like this is shared, it's mandatory that people be empathetic and supportive. A host's openness is an opportunity to gently probe these great pains. "Can you tell us more about your son?" we might question. In fact, it's not at all out of place to stop and pray for the individual that very moment.

More and more frequently, we are using our brunch time to comment on what the morning service means to us and how we see ourselves applying the lessons being taught. For most of the participants, this is a new experience. And wouldn't you know it, the 8:00 A.M. service is growing!

OPEN-HEART HOSPITALITY

Now, perhaps you've guessed where I'm headed and already you're thinking that weekends are impossible times for you to host a get-together. Or maybe you've already decided that your home is too small, too untidy, has too many stairs . . . that you can't cook, you have no furniture, or your utensils are made of plastic. I've found the key is not so much opening your home (even though that's very important) as it is opening your heart. In other words, you must truly be concerned about people and the distresses and joys of their lives. This kind of open-heart hospitality can be given whether you're sitting on the floor and eating with your fingers or moving boxes of papers off the table to make room for the carry-out bags. If someone at the table has a burden, you need to do your best to help lift it. If someone has experienced a great victory, you must truly rejoice in what God has done in that life. And I speak from experience when I say the effort is worth it.

Our pastor is going to be out of town in another month, and one of the church members has been asked to preach in his absence. This is a young man with a keen interest in being ordained someday. Last Sunday he shared with the group the text he has been assigned and said that he was struggling trying to figure out how to apply it. An older member at the table mentioned that a former pastor had preached on the exact same passage of Scripture. She had found it a very meaningful message and talked for a good five minutes about a sermon she had heard some 25 years before. I sat there absolutely amazed! Her testimony emphasized how the Lord truly speaks through sermons. How wonderful it was that this young minister-wannabe was there to hear and hopefully to someday be a part of the ongoing preaching miracle.

Another participant of our Sunday brunches is working on a doctoral degree. The other day she told me, "For a long time I haven't really looked forward to church all that much. But this weekly time with others in various homes has made everything different for me. Now I am eagerly anticipating Sundays—and that's a huge change!"

> **THE KEY: CHRISTIANS WEARY OF SUPERFICIAL RELATIONSHIPS ARE ENERGIZED WHEN WE OPEN OUR HOMES AND OUR HEARTS.**

If I put her comments in my own words I would say that Christian hospitality is one of the great untapped miracles the church needs to rediscover. *Christians weary of superficial relationships are energized by the significant connections that develop when we open our homes and our hearts.*

A graduate student from mainland China is away in

Boston on a special job. She had attended several of our church brunches, and I received a letter from her saying she missed these times. She had come to our country hoping to learn what real American people are like and had not been able to experience this except in our little brunch group, so she was looking forward to coming back for more of this interaction and discovering what was happening with these brothers and sisters in Christ. My great fear is that my Chinese friend could have attended most North American churches for several years and never would have had access to this kind of ongoing invitation.

This delight in getting to know people may be the main difference between Mary and Martha in that famous chapter where Jesus came to their home. How wonderful that they practiced hospitality and were able to have the Son of God himself as a guest. Unfortunately, Martha was more taken up with the busywork of making sure everything turned out just right. That's the problem with what we call *entertainment*. The focus is on ourselves, our homes, and our presentations. But Mary chose the better option. She decided to focus on her Lord. She opted for *hospitality*. And I believe the time was not only meaningful to her, but to the Lord as well.

LOVING AND ACCEPTING

Not long ago, one of our writer/producers and her husband and children were guests for dinner. Karen fixed a marvelous meal, but one of the little girls would have nothing to do with it. My wife's response? She opened the cupboards, saying, "Nobody is coming to my house and going away hungry! What would you enjoy eating?" It turned out that peanut butter and jelly was a favorite, so Karen fixed a sandwich and put it on the little one's plate. Her mother stopped by later to thank me for that gesture. Instead of having to feel embarrassed by her child's picky eating habits, she related how loved and accepted they all felt when Karen graced her beautifully prepared table with a peanut butter jar. Again, what was most important was the comfort and the good feelings of the guests (both the parents and the children), not a need for the host to be puffed by praise.

I don't believe we can ever get the contemporary church to return to holding its services in homes. That idea presents other problems that could result in huge headaches. But it's certainly possible to rethink the use of our homes as places of ministry ancillary to what goes on in the "official" church facility.

What I'm suggesting fits so beautifully with the theme of the previous chapter about being 24/7 Christians. Our faith must not be confined to a given building or time slot. We need to learn to be Christians who use both our gifts and our resources in manifold ways to bring glory to Christ and his kingship.

Let's return for a moment to David Letterman and Jay Leno. In a way, it's not fair to compare their conversational skills with the kind of open-heart-and-home give and take I'm suggesting here. Why? Because they're entertainers. Entertaining and hospitality are nearly opposite. Talk-show hosts want the focus, no matter what the celebrity status of their guests may be. When a celebrity is too amusing, too much the center of attention, you can almost feel the host grabbing back the reins. Hospitality works the other way. The focus should always be on the guest, not on showcasing the host's talents, achievements, and possessions.

WHY NOT BE HOSPITABLE?

Because of our outspoken interest in the great value of Christian hospitality, through the years Karen and I have heard a lot of reasons (I might call them excuses!) for why people hesitate to get involved in this kind of outreach. Most of them relate to a basic misunderstanding of the key difference between entertaining and hospitality. Here are a few of the more typical comments we've heard with how a proper understanding can allay these concerns.

Reason #1: Our home just isn't ready for entertaining.

That's fine, because you're not entertaining, you're offering hospitality. Hospitality can be given at a picnic table, on a coffee table, or next to a ladder and half-empty cans of paint.

A friend laughed recalling the story of a time she invited an older couple over for dinner. This man and woman were former employers who had been known for their beautifully decorated home, but now they lived in a retirement center. Our friend was reluctant to extend the invitation because her husband was halfway through removing the wallpaper in their dining room—a project that had stalled when he got a new work assignment, which cut into weekends. Finally, she decided to invite them anyway, in spite of the blotchy walls. "Wouldn't you know it?" she told us, "I'm not sure whether they needed new glasses, were just being gracious, or thought it was a new style. The only thing they commented on was the pretty dining room and how wonderful it was to eat a home-cooked meal in such a nice atmosphere!"

Reason #2: I'm no good at making small talk.

Karen and I once invited a well-known Christian leader to a get-together at our home. He regaled the group with stories, shared witty anecdotes, and jumped in at every opportunity with his opinion on various subjects. Granted, he was entertaining. But he wasn't very hospitable to the rest of the group. When everyone went home, Karen and I realized we didn't know much more about our other guests' lives than when they'd arrived. We were saddened to have missed the opportunity to discover any struggles or concerns they might have been facing.

A college student once explained why he disliked talking to his father. He felt his father treated everything he said as mere punctuation in the father's own monologue. No matter what the son said, it didn't evoke a question or a response or a turn in the conversation. It merely made breathing room for the older man to rally strength and continue with his own agenda.

If you're awkward at telling jokes, horrible at remembering interesting stories, and evasive of small talk at parties, you can still offer life-changing, energizing hospitality to others. In fact, you may be better at it than the "life of the party" types. Arm yourself with a few good questions, then sit back and listen. Do what comes naturally—practice diffidence—and keep turning the spotlight back on your guest. The rest of us will watch and learn from you!

Reason #3: Nobody at church is in our age bracket or life circumstances.

Christian hospitality isn't just about collecting new friends or meeting people with common interests. It's not really about you at all, although I think you'll be amazed at how delightful it is to grow closer to someone in a different passage of life, from a foreign part of the world, or from a family entirely dissimilar to yours. Offering hospitality to people like this can be incredibly interesting and, yes, energizing. When the focus is off your own needs, wants, and criteria and on someone else instead, your prospective guest list will expand rapidly!

> "I COULDN'T BELIEVE IT! THEY ATE ON REAL PLATES, WITH JELL-O AND PEAS! I WAS SO IMPRESSED— JELL-O!"

You're retired, with no children of your own? Ask that young couple with the gaggle of little ones to join you for lunch on Saturday. You don't think they'd be interested? A woman thanked me profusely for the invitation we extended to her, her husband, and their three children. As she told me, "The world isn't very accepting of kids today. Some people treat them as invisible or only ask us over when we can get a baby-sitter. With three kids, whenever anybody asks us any-where, we say yes! And we were amazed at the way you got them to talk! Even our quiet one wanted his turn at those questions you asked!"

You have a big family of your own and little more to offer than an extra serving of tuna casserole? Great! Invite the college student who's eaten nothing but fast food for the last two weeks. At a brainstorming session on this topic of hospitality, a young mother recalled with great joy the time she was in college and received an invitation from a family at church. "I couldn't believe it! They ate on real plates, with Jell-O and peas! I was so impressed—Jell-O!" Today she has her own ministry of hospitality in her neighborhood.

You're single and your table only seats two? Invite an older person, a foreign exchange student, or a visiting missionary. When only one person comes to your party, you may be failing according to the standards of secular entertaining. But when it comes to hospitality, a quiet, one-on-one conversation is probably exactly what your guest is looking for.

Reason #4: I'm inexperienced. I don't know how to handle having company!

A few weeks ago, Karen and I were out of town, and another couple from our church hosted the traditional Sunday brunch. The next week the husband told me how well it had gone. "In fact," he commented, "folks got there at 9:30 and a few didn't leave until 1:30! What do you do about that?" Jokingly, I suggested he could get into his pajamas and announce he was taking a Sunday afternoon nap. After we laughed, I told him it's okay to set parameters on your invitation. When you invite people over, for example, you can mention that the get-together will last until noon. "Hey, that's a great idea for next time," he responded, "but at least I know when everyone hangs around they were having a great time, right?" Right. Focusing on the needs and lives of your guests is what's most important.

Another tip my wife gives to potential hosts is to team up with a friend or fellow church member. If you've never had people into your home, ask someone else to serve as your mentor. Invite a more experienced host from your church to walk you through the steps. Ask for ideas and volunteers from your Sunday school class. And relax! Consider it a part of your ministry to *never* do a perfect hosting job—it only discourages others from trying to match what they've just experienced. As time goes on, you'll get more comfortable and even more creative in your approach.

HUNGRY FOR FELLOWSHIP

We recently tried something new with our Sunday brunch group. Our minister isn't able to come to these gatherings following the 8:00 service because, of course, he has to lead a 10:00 service, which is the larger of the two. Anxious that he not feel excluded, we arranged for a Saturday night meal in which numbers of the early service people could get together with him and share what's happening. The responsibility was divided by assigning various people to bring different dishes. We decided to pattern our time together after a Jewish

Sabbath meal, a Lord's Day Eve tradition our family has developed over the years. In order not to be too complicated, we only emphasize a few elements from the more elaborate traditional Sabbath Friday night ceremony.

For example, in a Jewish home, the children always know that on Sabbath Eve they will receive a blessing from the father or mother. The parent places hands on each son or daughter and shares a desire or prayer for him or her. Maybe the child is complimented about some positive quality. Perhaps the parent suggests a possible future path the child might take because of the fine characteristics he or she possesses.

So we exchanged names between the group members who were expected at the Saturday meal. Then we had a beautiful time of pronouncing blessings over one another, including our pastor and his family. Once again, this is an attempt to make the evening together something more than just a time to eat. Our primary hope is that through special occasions like these, people will become more aware of the sweet presence of the risen Lord in our midst.

I'm not sure I've been able to do justice to what actually takes place at these times together. But they are truly remarkable, and I am convinced they are the kind of fellowship so many people hunger for in our world and, yes, in our churches. I know friends enjoy conversations that are more than surface talk. In fact, I would go so far as to say most people would make a wise decision between:

1. Getting together to watch David Letterman or Jay Leno in action, with them talking to some of the famous

people of the world. The conversation would probably be spicy, and when the show was over, those who gathered would no doubt talk about how neat it was to hear such-and-such a person's views.

Or—

2. Going to God's house and experiencing what it's like to be a part of the body of Christ in corporate worship, and then enjoying a time of hospitality in a Christian home. Brunch might be served and people would speak about Jesus—what he meant to them especially and how the theme of the morning related to their walk of faith. There's a good chance you would join in prayer with others and experience the presence and love of the risen Christ.

Which of the two options do you prefer? One might be more entertaining. But the other would put you, your unique needs and concerns, and your relationship with the living God at the center of attention.

AN ASSIGNMENT: TRY IT!

It's wonderful to be on the receiving end of Christian hospitality. Trust me when I tell you it's even more wonderful to extend it. That's why I have an assignment for you, which promises to unleash an untapped miracle in your life, providing remarkable spiritual energy to both you and others in your church.

Over the next few weeks, consider how God can use your home and how you can open your heart to others. You don't have to start by hosting a weekly brunch. Remember, Karen and I have had years of experience in this area of hospitality and believe it is one in which

God has gifted us. However, I'm certain most people are able to invite others into their home for coffee, dessert, or a simple meal.

Let God take the lead. Talk to him about whom to welcome. It could be a single individual, a couple, a family, or a group of folks from different walks of life. Some people getting started simply make an extra serving or two for Saturday or Sunday dinner, then ask God to show them who they can invite home after church for a meal.

When you make your plans, follow these simple steps:

> IT'S WONDERFUL TO BE ON THE RECEIVING END OF HOSPITALITY. TRUST ME WHEN I TELL YOU IT'S EVEN MORE WONDERFUL TO EXTEND IT.

1. Don't emphasize the food you serve or the way your house looks. Remember Jesus' gentle words to the busy Martha in Luke 10:41 (NIV): "Martha, Martha . . . only one thing is needed. Mary has chosen what is better." It's okay to want to serve, as Martha did. But if you start grumbling and complaining about it, you know something is wrong. Stop and focus on really being there with your guests, as Mary did.

2. Put time beforehand into making sure the conversation is truly meaningful, including some way to minister to one another. Prepare several good questions—ones that can't be answered with a simple yes or no.

3. If you're unable to open your own home, cohost

a get-together with someone else. Maybe you could provide some of the food or volunteer to take on the task of delegating responsibilities for a potluck meal. If you absolutely can't find a home to meet in, gather a group at a nearby restaurant or picnic facility. Simply use the open-heart principles I've outlined in this chapter.

Getting back to that decision between listening in on a Leno or Letterman conversation and a gathering with others in a warm, hospitable Christian home—the only reason people might make the wrong choice is because they are more familiar with Letterman and Leno. But they might have a hard time picturing the beauty of what Christian hospitality has to offer because they've never experienced it the way it should be.

This has to change! And as it does, you'll see how making connections with others can revitalize your sense of community and spark the fire of your spirit. Believe me, if that's not a miracle, I don't know what is. It's absolutely true, as my wife writes in her book, *Open Heart, Open Home:* "In this inhospitable world, a Christian home is a miracle to be shared."

CHAPTER FOUR

UNTAPPED MIRACLE

4

PULPIT/PEW MUTUAL SUPPORT

A COMMON JOY

by Greg Asimakoupoulos

Weary from his task,
Moses asked
those he'd taken the time
to understand
to stand for a time under him.
And with helping hands
they shared the load,
supporting their shepherd
(and his staff).
A lesson here, methinks.
When they who lead
and they who follow
swallow pride to be a team,
their dreams become a common joy,
and their burdens become half.

When progress on any given front comes to a halt, it's time to think in terms of a breakthrough.

Maybe it's a business where foreign competition is capturing more and more of the market share. To continue taking the company along the same course without changes will probably be traveling a fast road to oblivion. Some kind of breakthrough is needed in strategy, production, or marketing.

In the early days of the automotive industry, a single individual or team put an entire vehicle together, from fuel pump to hubcaps. Eventually, quality and productivity were holding steady, but not increasing. Then Henry Ford implemented the idea of the moving assembly line. That breakthrough affected not only how cars were made; it was studied and copied by manufacturers around the world.

In conventional warfare, opposing generals looked for a breakthrough in the troop line of the enemy. Once they found it, they quickly attempted to capitalize on this breach as a way to move into new territory.

Even in noncombative disciplines like the arts, breakthroughs are commonly acknowledged. For example, painting styles continued unchanged for long years until certain artists broke new ground. Impressionists like Monet and Renoir broke out of the status quo style of realism and instead painted their overall impressions of a subject or scene. They didn't pay as much attention to details as had been the custom, and their style was a recognized breakthrough.

The same has been true in music. The traditionalist may ask, "What's wrong with how we've been doing things?" But a Debussy feels his creativity is being hemmed in. So he takes a different approach, and a new classical style is born.

In the church world today, we see this happening in

the area of worship. The manner in which the present generation expresses its faith musically stands in stark contrast to that of earlier generations. And regardless of whether you think new musical worship styles are good or bad, there's no question that a massive breakthrough has occurred.

Now, I'm of the opinion that in our day we need to see another breakthrough in the Christian world, and it's in the area of pulpit/pew relationships. What's wrong with how we've been doing things up till now? Well, for far too many people, Sunday morning has become a "been there, done that" tedium. It's not that they've stopped attending church, it's just that many of them have stopped expecting anything new or significant to occur. Thank the Lord this is not true everywhere. But in numerous settings, the services are much too predictable, and a growing number of people have lost the sense of enthusiasm and expectancy they used to bring with them to church. Let's be honest—how hyped are most parishioners about listening to another sermon or homily? And how excited is the average minister about preparing another message?

COMMUNICATIONS BREAKTHROUGHS

This impasse has been created in part by changing communication styles throughout North America. We're no longer a lecture-oriented culture. The styles that influence most people today are story telling and interview.

Think about it. Stories were what helped fuel the sexual revolution of the '60s and '70s. Plenty of sermons were preached defending God's views of human sexuality. But movies and television dramas won the day. The scripts for these films, made-for-TV features, and episodes of *Love American Style* weren't necessarily honest or complete. They never told what happened to "what's-her-name" when the movie hero left her for someone new he'd found more attractive or personally fulfilling. The story lines seldom dealt with the lives of children or showed what the hot new relationship looked like three years after the adultery took place. But they did convince people that passionate feelings should be pursued. And once the gentle romantic music started in the background, from that point on we were led to assume everything somehow turned out wonderful.

The truth is, during this same time period church people also had powerful stories to tell about matters of love. Christian men and women were tempted sexually, but they choose to remain true to their marriage vows. These conflicts had all the necessary built-in tension to make for good tales. But instead of telling their stories, church people pretended they didn't have such problems, or that romantic difficulties weren't worth talking about, or that plots favoring fidelity weren't really all that significant. We had the message to share, but we chose to ignore the breakthrough communication method that continues to rule the day.

Interviews also have a profound impact on the way people presently think. Who hasn't watched Oprah and Geraldo, or Donahue, Rafael, and Rosie, to name a few. But we in the church still haven't learned how to publicly ask our people the kinds of questions that unlock a view of what the Lord is doing in believers' lives. We've chosen to ignore the fact that in days past, the Lord used people sharing their testimonies to prompt revival almost as often as he used preaching.

INPUT BREAKTHROUGHS

Another major innovation that has taken place in recent generations is the great value placed on collaborative work. Most contributions of importance are no longer the efforts of just one individual. Yet in the church, we still rely on ministers doing all the work on their sermons with almost no input from others either before, during, or after they are delivered. If we expect the church to take on new vitality, we'll need a breakthrough here, too.

What drives most successful enterprises today is a good relationship between the producer and the consumer. If no attention is paid to what the customer is thinking, before long a business is going to be in trouble. Yet in the church, almost no input is requested or given by those attending about what they find helpful and what they don't need. As a result, the best thing the church has going for it is loyalty. And like it or not, the younger generation doesn't hold that quality as high as older people do.

Wouldn't it be something if there could be a breakthrough in this area of pulpit/pew relationships? I'm not thinking of anything critical or destructive. What I'm envisioning would be a win/win scenario, with everyone moving forward into new territory. As a speaker, if a service is boring, I want to know why so I can work to make it more interesting. If my sermon isn't touching people where they live, it only makes sense that they have a constructive way to make suggestions for improvement. And I also need to know congregation members are there for me—in prayer and other ways—when I need them. What I'm talking about is mutual support between those who stand in the pulpit and those who sit in the pew.

PREACHING PARTNERSHIPS

Of all the books I've read through the years, one that's on my Most Helpful List was written back in 1967 by Reuel Howe. Titled *Partners in Preaching*, it wasn't a big seller, but over the years I have probably reviewed it at least eight to ten times. I'm convinced the author struck on an idea before its time, because what he wrote is still incredibly relevant for the needs of the church today.

In the book, Howe interviewed large numbers of people on their feelings about sermons. He found that almost unanimously, lay people felt the typical sermon contained too many ideas. These came at them so fast and in such a complex fashion that it was next to impossible to keep any one of them in mind long enough to relate it to what was happening in their lives. As early as my first pastorate, I found this discovery consistent with what people were telling me.

That's why during my years in the local church, I used to schedule a discussion group following every Sunday morning service. Then whoever wanted to could sit with me and discuss what I had just preached about. I would usually begin by asking people to put into a sentence what they heard as the central thrust of my sermon. One day, after those in attendance had a great deal of trouble coming up with such a summary, one participant commented, "Pastor, why don't *you* try to put into a sentence what it is you were trying to say?" I struggled to do so and eventually gave up in frustration.

That was a turning point in my ministry. After that experience, I always tried to reduce what I wanted to say to a key sentence. This became a habit whether I was talking to a congregation, preparing a video broadcast, lecturing a class of students, or writing a book. For example, the idea I'm emphasizing in this chapter is: *In order for the worship service's been-there, done-that tedium to change, a breakthrough is needed in pulpit/pew relationships.*

Before we go further, I need you to hear me say that I'm probably going to be writing mostly to pastors at first. It will look like ministers are the ones to initiate these breakthroughs. But parishioners, don't immediately cheer too loudly, because your turn for making some important changes is coming up in just a few pages!

OPENING FEEDBACK LINES

One of those initial breakthroughs I'm referring to is the establishment of better lines of communication between pulpit and pew. That was the basic premise of *Partners in Preaching*. Reuel Howe felt that the best judges of sermons were not seminary professors, but plumbers and housewives and bus drivers and anyone who listened to preaching week after week. These people knew intuitively whether or not the sermon they'd heard offered something of value. Unfortunately, these kinds of folks are seldom given a forum to relate how they are or aren't being helped.

The television industry spends "beaucoup bucks" finding out what viewers think. Go to a shopping center and chances are, you'll be stopped by someone with a clipboard who wants to ask a few questions on behalf of the mall management. That's because sounding out customers' responses is recognized as critically important. But in the church, and especially with sermons, we're more prone to treat nonclergy responses as unwelcome.

> **THE KEY:**
> IN ORDER FOR THE WORSHIP SERVICE'S BEEN-THERE, DONE-THAT TEDIUM TO CHANGE, A BREAKTHROUGH IS NEEDED IN PULPIT/PEW RELATIONSHIPS.

Howe felt it was crucial for congregations to be given a way to give feedback about the sermons they heard. This wasn't to be done in a negative manner. But certainly parishioners needed an opportunity to express what they found helpful. As a minister, when I finish speaking I don't want to see people acting like Olympic judges, holding up cards for the high divers with a ranking of 1–10. On the other hand, I understand how I could be helped by hearing people say what was of most value to them. A letter or a phone call with that kind of information would certainly be appreciated.

Even more importantly, Howe felt it would be beneficial for ministers to regularly go over their sermon ideas with representatives from the congregation—

prior to preaching them. When I put this concept into practice in my own ministry, I found it an incredibly helpful exercise. Yes, at first it was intimidating. Over time, however, it became a step in the preparation process I couldn't do without.

I remember some of those early get-togethers with lay people from the church. Usually the meetings would be for an early breakfast on a Monday or Tuesday before my congregation members hurried on to work. These men and women were always gentle in their response to my ideas, but I quickly began to understand that we were at different places spiritually. My suggestions were usually beyond what they felt themselves capable of doing. My Bible knowledge was unnerving, and my manner of living was different from theirs. They had to battle hard for time to pray, to read Scripture, and to share their faith. These were activities they saw me being paid to do.

More than once I heard comments like:

◆ "You're assuming I'm more advanced spiritually than I really am."
◆ "That point might work, Pastor, but only if you had a congregation of people who were all professional ministers!"
◆ "Can't you use more illustrations of people who live in the real world instead of telling so many stories about spiritual men like Matthew Henry or Charles Spurgeon or D. L. Moody?"
◆ "Please don't imagine that when you give a huge challenge like developing a love for God's Word, we

can do it in the following week. And we can't real-istically be ready to then take on another challenge of equal or even greater magnitude by the follow-ing week."

◆ "Talk to me about more earthy matters. What if I'm married and I have a crush on someone at work?

◆ "How do I start giving money to the church when I can't even make ends meet now?"

◆ "How do I resist being jealous of congregation members who obviously were given a better head start on life than I was?"

◆ "Your family represents several generations of Christians. You mustn't assume we share that same privilege."

I need to underscore that these discussions with parishioners energized my preaching. They made me aware that people were listening and truly wanted answers to their questions. They helped me feel sup-ported, like my role as pastor was one of great value to them. But they also caused me to realize I wasn't doing as effective a job as I would have wished.

Apparently the discussions also energized my parishioners. Those who participated in the sermon brainstorming sessions showed greater interest in what I preached. Participants frequently offered suggestions on the topics we talked about together, and they started telling me they were praying for me. (That sure felt good.) Usually the first people to say a given message was helpful were those who had been involved in the presermon meetings. Most of all, they seemed excited when I used an idea they had come up with!

In the ten years I spent in my last pastorate, I had hundreds of people involved in such dialogues. They were the ones who were most highly supportive of my ministry, and over the years I came to greatly value the kind of input they provided.

Once when interviewed on a Christian radio show, I was asked to name my favorite set of commentaries. My reply was, "My parishioners." At first my answer didn't make sense to the program host, so I explained what I meant. We must have talked for five to ten minutes about that one point. This radio personality was absolutely dumbfounded that any minister would do such a thing as meet with people to plan sermons. Again, I gave credit to Reuel Howe for the original idea, but this media person made it clear that wherever the thought came from, it was a real bell-ringer as far as he was concerned.

PRAYER PARTNERSHIPS

A second area where we need to see a breakthrough in pulpit/pew relationships relates to prayer. Because of the present "great divide" between pastors and parishioners, I'm convinced that consistent prayer support isn't happening as it should. In fact, this is undoubtedly one of the major reasons ministers are worn out and unable to rally the troops the way they would like.

A young mother with two or three small children knows what it's like to have days slip away without feeling like she's accomplished all that much. Getting the daily chores done at the same time she's trying to keep the kids happy and out of trouble is a full-time job in itself. Thank the Lord for grandparents or friends who help out on occasion. If this same woman works part-time, takes classes toward a degree, finds occasion to write poetry, or teaches a weekly Christian education class, she is seldom appreciated by others the way she deserves. And who prays for a young mom who volunteers for one of the many jobs needing to be filled at the church?

WHEN I ASK PEOPLE IF THEY COVER THEIR MINISTERS IN PRAYER, MOST ADMIT IT'S UNUSUAL FOR THEM TO DO THIS.

As strange as it sounds, I found that being a pastor was somewhat similar. Far too many jobs to do—"Can't we find anybody to take charge of Vacation Bible School this year?" Routines repeated over and over—"What premarital session number is this, Marge (my secretary), and can you remember the names of the couple coming to the office to see me?" So many new Christians to care for—"Thank the Lord for spiritual births, but babies require a lot of attention!" A profusion of unrealistic expectations—"As a clergy couple, we like having people from the church over. But we just can't get around to everyone—it's impossible to fit another social night into our schedule—and now several of our members feel neglected!"

When I was pastoring, sometimes the various meetings and the people and the days all got confused, and before I knew it, it was time to preach again. Yet did anyone realize how much last week's sermon took out of me?

As a grandparent, I know that my daughter or daughter-in-law always appreciate a call asking, "What can I do to help?" I'm also conscious of what it means for them to hear, "I prayed for you and your kids this morning." This short conversation would minister to pastors as well: "Anything I can do to be of help, Pastor? Maybe I could just listen and be impressed by all you have to do today. Can I also carry you in prayer regarding a special need, a looming deadline, or a tough decision? Do you have time for me to pray for you over the phone right now?"

My observation is that pastors aren't prayed for as much as they should be. When I ask people if they cover their ministers in prayer, most admit it's unusual for them to do this. Their reason is that prayer isn't that much a part of their lives to begin with. And when they do pray, it's usually for more immediate personal concerns. On top of this, they're not sure what they would say to the Lord if they brought up their pastor's name. For most parishioners, praying about their minister's sermons is a concept that's totally foreign to them.

I don't want to make excuses for something we all know we should be doing. But if congregation members aren't somehow involved in the sermon conception, it's no wonder they've dropped completely out of the sermonizing process.

Author Terry Teykl, pastor of the Aldersgate United Methodist Church in College Station, Texas, has written an excellent book called *Preyed On or Prayed For.* The subtitle is *Hedging Your Pastor in Prayer.* He writes that the seven areas in your pastor's life and ministry most likely to come under attack are his or her (1) private life, (2) family life, (3) praise life, (4) prayer life, (5) professional life, (6) preaching life, and (7) persevering life.

Teykl makes a strong case for the importance of pastors working aggressively to build a prayer hedge around themselves. To do this, clergy members must share specific information as to what their prayer needs are. Then, feedback on how the Lord is answering these prayer requests also has to be given. Involvement needs to be encouraged from the pulpit because the prayer role is central to all that takes place in a church. I love the way Teykl draws on the Old Testament picture of Moses, Aaron, and Hur. "In Exodus 17, Pastor Moses is having a hard time," Teykl writes. "The Israelites are short of water and they blame Moses, their pastor! The people call a meeting of the B.T.E. (Back to Egypt) Committee to grumble against Moses." Then he goes on to describe how God provided water from the rock at Rephidim and the "B.T.E. Committee" adjourned.

> Moses probably thought his troubles were over. But just as everyone settles down, the Amalekites attack. Pastor Moses orders Joshua into battle and takes Aaron and Hur to the top of the hill to pray. As Moses watches the battle, he lifts his hands over the people. We read that as long as Moses held up his hands, the Israelites were winning, but whenever he lowered his hands, the Amalekites were winning.
>
> As the battle continues, Aaron and Hur notice that Moses' hands are growing tired, and

they quickly discern the danger this might cause the Israelites. So Aaron and Hur took a stone, sat their pastor on it between them, and held up his weary hands. Verse 12 says that Moses' hands "remained steady till sunset." The end result was a victory for the people of God! What a beautiful demonstration of support for a tired, battle-worn pastor.

Who is holding up your pastor's hands?

It's been said that the bigger the problem, the more wondrous will be the breakthrough solution. Well, this is a big problem: Ministers aren't supported by church people praying for them the way they should. But that can change, and when it does, I'm certain it will be wondrous!

HOW TO WORK THE MIRACLE

Before I share some specific suggestions on how you can start that process in your church, I want to add a quick word of counsel especially to those on the "pew" side of this equation. Through the years I've met thousands of local church pastors, and almost without exception I've found them sincere, hardworking, and deeply caring about the spiritual growth of their congregations. I've also discovered that many of them are hurting because they don't feel supported by their people. A smaller, yet still significant number are what I call "walking wounded" clergy members who are in genuine spiritual and emotional pain because of the constant criticism they face from those within their congregations.

Pulpit/pew mutual support can only bring about

positive change when the relationship is built on love and trust. If your pastor has never heard a good word about her preaching, don't expect her to readily open her office for a discussion on next week's sermon. If he's been criticized for the way his children behave, don't anticipate a prayer request from him for his son who's struggling in school. I doubt even Moses would have allowed Aaron and Hur to hold up his arms if he had been fearful about them taking a quick shot at his exposed midsection!

The breakthrough I'm proposing, the one that can energize the worship service experience for both you and your pastor, can only come when you work together. This isn't about pushing your pastor in the direction you want him or her to go. It's not about your pastor expecting you to learn Hebrew and Greek so the sermons will be more appreciated. This is about the two of you—pulpit and pew—working together to take steps in a brand new direction. This isn't a tug of war. It's walking side by side to break through into an exciting new area of spiritual ground you've never stepped foot on before.

So how do you begin? Start right away to pray for your pastor before and during the sermon. Ask God to help you hear his message for you through your pastor's words.

When that happens—when you hear God speaking through the sermon, a particular Bible passage, or even the pastoral prayer—think of ways you can specifically apply what's been said to your day-to-day life. Put your pastor's words into action.

Now let's take this one more step. Jot a note, make a

phone call, or send an e-mail message to your pastor. Begin by sharing how you've been working to put the words he or she shares each week into practice. Then take the opportunity to offer your pastor some insights into your everyday life and what you need to hear. Some thoughts to include are:

- ◆ A way you've influenced my life is . . .
- ◆ Something you said that I've put into action is . . .
- ◆ A question I have is . . .
- ◆ If you could speak about . . . , that would be helpful to me.

Again, this isn't the time to offer negative criticism of your pastor's preaching, leadership style, the last all-church meeting, or the way the church grounds are being kept. This is your opportunity to help your pastor better understand your needs, and to start the breakthrough process that ends in a stronger pulpit/pew relationship.

What if sitting through sermons you have trouble following were a thing of the past? Would that be significant? Sure it would!

What if a minister never again had to fear losing an audience he or she was addressing? Wouldn't that be something? Of course!

Those are exactly the kinds of changes that can result from pulpit/pew mutual support.

A composer, author, graphic artist, sportswriter, graduate student working on a thesis—anyone who's tried to create something from scratch—has mental blocks sooner or later. That's one of those awful occasions when everything shuts down and you don't know whether or not you'll be able to finish the job at hand. You stall and hope that after the intervening time you will eventually produce something of value. Would you believe that most ministers face this same problem more frequently than they care to admit? I know that's true. I speak with preachers more than with any other professional group, and this problem comes up frequently.

> WHAT THESE PAS-TORS NEED IS SOME KIND OF MIRACLE THEY CAN TAP INTO THAT WILL START THE CREATIVE JUICES FLOWING ONCE AGAIN.

What these pastors need is a breakthrough—some kind of miracle they can tap into that will start the creative juices flowing once again. They also need a wonder potion that makes them aware of how loved they are. And that, of course, is exactly what I'm writing about in this chapter.

Listen. I'm telling you that sometimes a clergy person can sit at a word processor for three or four hours straight and have little to show for it. Wouldn't it be a much better investment of time to call a parishioner or two and ask, "How does this passage I'm working on relate to you? From your perspective, what's clear about it and what isn't? Does it touch on anything you're presently facing? Would you do me a favor and read it again tonight and then meet with me and a couple of others from the church for an early breakfast tomorrow morning? I'm trying to put together this week's sermon, and I need your input."

On the other hand, a member of the congregation could just as easily call a minister and ask, "What topic are you preaching on this week, Pastor? I'm really having trouble with this area of my life, and I'm hoping sometime soon you can address this. By the way, I want you to know I care deeply about what you do, and because of that I'm praying for you every day this week."

See, I'm writing about a miracle that hasn't been tapped into the way it could or should be. It's the excitement of working collaboratively on a job that's bigger than any one person. It's pastors and parishioners getting into one another's worlds through the miracle of dialogue. It's not really as impossible or as scary as it might sound at first. It just takes a couple of people nodding their heads and saying, "Sounds like a good idea. We should explore supporting one another."

It's the miracle breakthrough of pulpit/pew mutual support. And who knows? Someday you might even become a part of your pastor's favorite set of commentaries!

CHAPTER FIVE

UNTAPPED MIRACLE
5

PRAYER WITH FASTING

FEED ME, FATHER

by Greg Asimakoupoulos

Hearing you speak
is too hard
too often,
Father.
I know what it takes,
but life is
too loud,
too busy, and
too fast
to fast and pray.

Please pass the desire
to deny myself
when I feel like a meal
is all I need
to fill my emptiness.
Feed me,
Father,
feed me

with a double portion
of your Spirit,
a cup of silence,
and a slice
of the Bread of Life.

I want to fast
to slowly chew your grace.

I have no doubt grapevines must contribute to the good of the world. But for most of my junior year in high school, I wanted as little to do with them as possible!

As a sophomore, I had gone out for the high school wrestling team, but I was never good enough to wrestle for my weight class in an actual event. During the summer, however, the teammate who always beat me put on some extra pounds. So for my junior year, I was suddenly the school's number-one contender in my weight classification. How excited I was to actually be representing our Blue Devil squad when we went up against . . . *Wood River*. Now, to recapture what those two words meant to us, you need to read them out loud with a little tremble in your voice. Wood River. This tough Mississippi River town located just above St. Louis always had a couple of state champions on their squad.

I don't recall my opponent's name, but my coach told me to be careful not to let him get me in a grapevine. Apparently he had used it against our team members on several earlier occasions. Whenever this guy was behind you, he would quickly throw his right leg around your stomach and speedily tuck that foot under the bend of his left leg. This meant your middle was in a tight leg hold. While you were still worrying about your tummy, his second step was to get your arms trapped above your head, leaving you defenseless. Then with great pleasure, he would squeeze his legs and slowly rock your entire body back and forth, all the time moving your shoulders closer and closer to the mat. The grapevine was almost impossible to get out of. But if you exerted great effort and really fought it, you might keep your shoulders from being pinned.

All the matches started with both wrestlers standing, but would you believe that within 30 seconds, I was on the mat locked in this fellow's famous grip? This meant I had to struggle and strain for a full minute and a half just to extend the match into period two. Because this was my first bout and a high school girl I really liked was watching, I did my best to keep my shoulders from being held down for the humiliating three count. It seemed like an eternity of pain. But I was finally rescued by the official timer.

Next it was my turn to start on top, and I must have maintained this dominant position for at least 15 seconds. Okay, maybe 10 seconds! Even though this Strangler Louis protégé slipped free from my advantage, I was sure of one thing—he wasn't going to get me in that same hold again. But somehow, with amazing speed, he grapevined me again, and once more it was my fate to somehow try to keep one shoulder off the mat. Only the Lord knows how I managed until period two was finally over.

When it was his turn to start out on top, I remember my coach yelling that I was way behind on points and now the only way I could win was to pin him. There wasn't adequate time for my fearless leader to explain what kind of miracle he had in mind. All I knew was that I was extremely tired, and while I may have been the same weight as this incredible human wrestling machine, I wasn't in his class.

> AS FAR AS I WAS CONCERNED, A NEWFANGLED "GRAPEVINE CLIPPER" OF SOME SORT WOULD HAVE BEEN PERFECT.

The whistle blew, and we were at it again. In almost no time he got that same accursed hold on me. He was certain I wouldn't survive this final round. Surprise—I did! But it was only because that pretty girl kept watching. Later I heard her joking about how funny it was to see me get suckered into that same predicament three times in a row. If I had known she felt that way, I would have given up without going through so much humiliating torture.

Such situations provoke teenage dreams of a secret weapon that will suddenly even things out a bit more. As far as I was concerned, a new-fangled "grapevine clipper" of some sort would have been perfect. Maybe that's what Mike Tyson was thinking when he bit the ear of heavyweight boxing champion Evander Holyfield.

Most people don't have the tenacity to keep going against impossible odds. One who had the kind of dogged persistence needed in such situations is Jean Valjean, the hero in the hit musical *Les Miserables.* Jailed for stealing bread to give a hungry child, Valjean is finally released from prison after 19 long years. His nemesis, Inspector Javert, claims, "Once a criminal, always a criminal."

"You'll be back, #24601!" he tells Valjean scornfully, even refusing him the dignity of being called by name. As the play develops, Javert repeatedly gets Valjean into his grapevine hold. Valjean's responsibility for raising a young orphan girl, Cosette, becomes his reason for continuing in this lifelong fight. The story of his eventual victory is superb, but it almost emotionally wears you out as you realize how strong Javert is.

In this chapter, I'd like to address what usually happens to people when they feel their enemy is stronger then they are. The fact is, after a while they get exhausted and more or less give up the fight. That's the way it is with both individual warriors and entire armies.

THE GREAT CHALLENGE

This truth also applies on the spiritual battlefield. When Satan always seems to have the bigger and better weapons, the troops get tired.

For example, it's hard to win battles against gambling now that the government has made its way into the business. How can one person fight what the state legislature has given its stamp of approval? In the same way, it's tough to fight the evils of abortion when the law protects what is going on. How do you raise sexually pure young men and women in a culture that leads them to believe virginity is something to be ashamed of? When psychics are legitimized by well-produced, half-hour infomercials, who are we to say that this is a trap to be avoided at all costs? And when violence is an entertainment staple, who's going to listen when we try to convince them that what's seen on the screen is bleeding out into everyday life?

This is a day when one church standard after another is being successfully challenged by the enemy of our souls. It can be exhausting for those who feel they're losing every battle. So I contend that it's time for God's people to reach out for a spiritual weapon with more fire power than their current arsenal has demonstrated. My firm belief is that the rediscovery of fasting will be exactly what we are looking for.

You'd be hard-pressed to find a Christian believer who doesn't believe in the power of prayer. The Scriptures clearly link the practice of fasting to intense prayer efforts, especially those involving spiritual battles against the enemy. Why, then, has this double-duty weapon of prayer and fasting gone untapped for so long in the North American church?

VICTORY BY FASTING

Recently our ministry went through several years of what I would call intense enemy fire. The details aren't all that important; suffice it to say it's a genuine miracle we survived the battle. I'm convinced one of the key reasons we did was because two young staff members fasted in our behalf, first for 20 consecutive days and then for another 40. In retrospect, I'm amazed at how the Lord walked us through our troubles. And while I'm not certain of the exact relationship between their fasting and how everything eventually worked out, I will always hold a conviction that the two were closely linked.

While preparing to launch into the topic of "Untapped Miracles for Tapped-out Christians," we held a retreat with a number of ministers who were instrumental in structuring the themes of this book and other corresponding materials. In one of our evening sessions, Dr. Lou Diaz, an Evangelical Free Church pastor, talked with the group. He told about what God had done in his life through a 40-day fast he had undertaken some months earlier. He's given his permission for me to recount a prayer he shared that outlines some of the reasons he gave for going on this fast:

> Lord Jesus, my purpose in fasting is to earnestly pray for spiritual awakening for the Church, especially our church, and for the fulfillment of your Great Commission. I am not using this time as a kind of hunger strike that compels you to do my bidding. I yield myself to you, desiring to know your will and to live in line with it. Yes, I want to express my love and worship to you. Yes, I want to humble myself before you. Yes, I want to express repentance for anything you reveal to me. Yes, I want to overcome temptation and dedicate myself to you. Yes, I want deliverance and protection. Yes, I am joining with others who attended the Fasting and Prayer Conference last November at the Los Angeles Convention Center to express concern for the work of God.
>
> Deep down inside me there is a longing to

break through a barrier of inconsistency about spiritual disciplines to a character-building consistency that seeks your face and knows your presence, power, and peace, on a higher plane than at present. I want to be a Christian who fully lives out my faith. I want to maximize my relationship and partnership with my wife, Shirley. I want to nurture my children, Laura and Stephen, in the way of the Lord, that they may know you and love you and serve you. I want you to be glorified in my life. I want to be the spiritual leader you want me to be. I want to be a vessel fit for noble purposes, useful to you. I want to see your bride beautiful and your body healthily functioning. I love your church, and I want her to be all you want her to be. I love the lost, and I want them to have an opportunity to know your great salvation. This is why I am fasting and praying.

Lou's presentation was challenging, and his manner was humble. He didn't come off as super-spiritual, and he didn't make us feel guilty for failing to match his effort. All of us were grateful for his openness, his honesty, and his enthusiasm for what the experience meant to him. He said he was a different man and a different minister because of this intense time of prayer and fasting.

Bob Rittenhouse, who heads our Canadian board of directors, was one of the ministers present when Lou shared his testimony. Several months later when I saw him in Canada, he told me how he, too, had just completed a 40-day fast. Inspired by what he had heard from this fellow pastor, he talked about how the discipline of fasting had revolutionized his life and ministry as well.

The Fasting and Prayer Conference mentioned by Lou Diaz was organized by Bill Bright, founder of Campus Crusade for Christ. Many men and women of our generation have been touched by Bill Bright's belief that the Lord will yet visit this nation in great revival power. Dr. Bright writes about his own experience with prayer and fasting for spiritual awakening in his book *The Coming Revival:*

> The longer I fasted, the more I sensed the presence of the Lord. The Holy Spirit refreshed my soul and spirit as never before. Biblical truths leaped at me from the pages of God's Word. My faith soared as I cried out to God and rejoiced in His presence.
>
> Early one morning after three weeks of fasting, I received the assurance from God that He would visit America in transforming, revival power. I found myself overcome with tears of gratitude. . . .
>
> As I knelt before the Lord at my favorite chair in our living room, I was sobered by the conditions that the Holy Spirit had placed on His promise to send revival. These conditions seemed to match the spirit of 2 Chronicles 7:14:
>
> *If my people, who are called by my name, will humble themselves and pray and seek my*

face and turn from their wicked ways, then will I hear from heaven and will forgive their sins and will heal their land.

With this Scripture strongly in my mind, I sensed the Holy Spirit was telling me that millions of believers must seek God with all of their hearts in fasting and prayer before He will intervene to save America. I was impressed by the Spirit to pray that two million believers will humble themselves by seeking God in forty-day fasts. (pp. 35, 37)

Dr. Bill Bright is a man of great faith. Today's church needs visionaries like him to call us to extraordinary responses. I believe the Lord will answer his prayer for two million Christians in North America who will fast for 40 days. I also believe this prayer commitment will make a huge difference regarding the future of our nation.

BREAKING THE DEATH GRIP

For most of us, however, a 40-day fast is a far too advanced initial step. So let me go back to a story in Scripture where a shorter fast broke a death grip Satan had on the people of God. Esther 3:12b–13 reads,

Letters were signed in the name of King Xerxes, sealed with his ring, and sent by messengers into all the provinces of the empire. The letters decreed that all Jews—young and old, including

women and children—must be killed, slaugh-
tered, and annihilated on a single day.

Think of what a similar decree against Christians
would mean today! How would you protect your children
and grandchildren?

Years earlier, the Lord in
his providence had brought
together two needy people. It
was a meeting not unlike that
of Jean Valjean and Cosette in
Les Miserables. In this case,
Mordecai had been taken prisoner following the fall of
Jerusalem to the Babylonians.

His tormentor was not
Javert, but the evil Haman, who
was a master "grapeviner."
What gave Mordecai reason to
live was a child he was raising—his cousin, who had lost
both her father and mother. When young Esther
matured and grew beautiful, she became the new queen
of the land. Here is how part of this fascinating Old
Testament narrative unfolds:

> **THE KEY:**
> WHEN IT SEEMS
> THE ENEMY
> ALWAYS HAS THE
> BIGGER AND
> BETTER WEAPONS,
> IT'S TIME FOR
> GOD'S PEOPLE
> TO GET SERIOUS
> ABOUT PRAYER
> BY FASTING.

> Then Esther sent for Hathach, one of the king's
> eunuchs who had been appointed as her atten-
> dant. She ordered him to go to Mordecai and find
> out what was troubling him and why he was in
> mourning. So Hathach went out Mordecai in the
> square in front of the palace gate.

Mordecai told him the whole story and told him how much money Haman had promised to pay into the royal treasury for the destruction of the Jews. Mordecai gave Hathach a copy of the decree issued in Susa that called for the death of all Jews, and he asked Hathach to show it to Esther. He also asked Hathach to explain it to her and to urge her to go to the king to beg for mercy and plead for her people. So Hathach returned to Esther with Mordecai's message.

Then Esther told Hathach to go back and relay this message to Mordecai, "The whole world knows that anyone who appears before the king without being invited is doomed to die unless the king holds out his gold scepter. And the king has not called for me to come to him in more than a month." So Hathach gave Esther's message to Mordecai.

Mordecai sent back this reply to Esther: "Don't think for a moment that you will escape there in the palace when all other Jews are killed. If you keep quiet at a time like this, deliverance for the Jews will arise from some other place, but you and your relatives will die. What's more, who can say but that you have been elevated to the palace for just such a time as this?"

Then Esther sent this reply to Mordecai: "Go and gather together all the Jews of Susa and fast for me. Do not eat or drink for three days, night or day. My maids and I will do the same. And then, though it is against the law, I

will go in to see the king. If I must die, I am
willing to die."

*When it seems the enemy always has the bigger and
better weapons, it's time for God's people to get serious
about prayer by fasting.* That's a lesson underscored in
many places in Scripture, certainly here in the Book of
Esther. The great series of victories that follows is
almost too good to be true. Be sure to read this book of
the Bible, because it will excite you to more seriously
consider fasting for some of the dilemmas facing the
church today.

ELIMINATE EXTREMES

But even a three-day fast is a bigger step then most
Christians have ever contemplated. In one of his sermons, John Wesley put into a sentence the dilemma I as
a novice feel while writing on this topic. He said, "Some
have exalted religious fasting beyond all Scripture and
reason; and others have utterly disregarded it."

Do you find yourself at one of those extremes? Or is
fasting a practice with which you have become comfortable? When it's appropriate, do you fast quite naturally?
Are you simultaneously careful to avoid the pattern of
the self-righteous Pharisee, who boasted to God in a
voice so loud others could hear (just as he wanted them
to) that he fasted twice a week (Luke 18:12)?

I know some people are afraid of fasting because it
smacks of asceticism. That word implies extreme self-
denial, and the stories are many of past Christians who
appeared to believe God took pleasure in their self-

imposed hardships and suffering. But asceticism is hardly the religious spirit of our age. On the contrary, what we manifest is more the extreme of wanting to be affirmed by God all the time, even entertained, but certainly not challenged to any kind of self-denial. In fact, I can imagine someone asking, "Why even bring up fasting in the first place? Why do we need it?"

Well, in the first place I bring it up so we can be more like Christ. You'll recall the account of our Lord's ministry begins with him fasting for 40 days in the wilderness. "Yes," you may respond, "but the Bible also states that Christ defended his disciples for not fasting."

> ASCETICISM IS HARDLY THE RELIGIOUS SPIRIT OF OUR AGE. ON THE CONTRARY, WE WANT TO BE AFFIRMED BY GOD, NOT CHALLENGED.

I agree. Matthew 9 is where that account is found. Jesus did stick up for the Twelve and their lack of conformity to Jewish expectations, but only for the time that he was here on earth. Our Lord's words were, "How can the guests of the bridegroom mourn while he is with them? The time will come when the bridegroom will be taken from them; then they will fast" (verse 15, NIV). I'd like to make the simple observation that the future time Jesus was referring to has obviously arrived. Fasting is now appropriate.

Secondly, I bring up this matter of fasting because I'm of the opinion the enemy has been winning far too many battles lately. I'm getting tired of struggling and stalling for no greater reward than a short rest before having to go at it again. And when back in the fray, too often I find the church is close to being pinned—again.

What's that the coach is yelling? We're going to have to finish strong if we want to have any hope of victory? And what miracle might he have in mind to make that possible? The grapevine *what*? Try the grapevine clippers? Such a thing really exists? Awesome!

WEAPON TRAINING

It's my sincere hope and prayer that the following suggestions will be read as much more than an informational overview on fasting. I want them to stand out like a Bill Bright–type challenge, which shouts that the time to get serious about fasting is *today.* I mean, how many mat burns do we need before we get the message that spiritually speaking, we need to turn things around—soon!

The very day Holyfield and Tyson sign a contract to box for the championship, their training begins. That's because getting into peak condition has a major impact on the outcome of the fight. We know we're already in a battle that's not going to get any easier. So when are we going to wise up and start training in the use of the Big Weapon we know we need? Our answer must be this week—this day, if possible. *Now* is the time for Christians to get serious about fasting and prayer.

Jesus battled the devil and soundly defeated him. Fasting was one of his key weapons. Now it's our turn. Here are some initial options for you to consider, even if you're a complete novice at this type of spiritual warfare:

1. The lunch-to-lunch juice fast.

This is the best entry-level option, and I highly recommend it for those who have not fasted before. Eat a healthy meal, including fruits and vegetables, for lunch one day. Then skip supper and breakfast, drinking only water and fruit juices (but not too much citrus). Break your fast joyfully next lunchtime. This two-meal fast could also go breakfast to breakfast or supper to supper, but the midday option is probably the easiest.

2. The three-meal fast.

If you've fasted before with good results, try a three-meal fast of about 30–36 hours—again drinking only fruit juice or water. Ideally, you would just pick a day and skip all meals. You should also alter other activities to concentrate on being with God in prayer.

3. The weekly two-meal or three-meal fast.

A number of Christians fast on a weekly basis. Every Wednesday or every Friday (or whichever day) is a fasting day for them.

4. Longer options.

Most experts do not recommend any fast longer than two or three meals, *unless you're an experienced faster.* If you know what you're doing, go for it. But make sure you consult your physician and a spiritual mentor or pastor. Your doctor can tell you how to make sure your body receives what's essential during your fast.

How you choose to *break* your fast is a very important health (and comfort) consideration. You don't want to start wolfing down food, or even going back to normal meals. Start slowly with foods that are easy on your stomach. Milk products are not recommended. Some people have found juices (not citrus), fruit (like watermelon and cantaloupe), vegetables, and broth, are good for breaking fasts. Then gradually work back to your normal eating pattern.

Note: There are some people who should *not* fast—pregnant and post-pregnant women, diabetics, heart patients, and those with such conditions as gout, liver disease, kidney disease, cerebral disease, pulmonary problems, tumors, bleeding ulcers, cancer, and blood disease. If you have any medical or psychological condition, or if you are taking any regular medication, please consult your doctor first. For these people, let me offer an alternative:

5. The replacement "fast."

Find some other habit that is nearly as central to your life as food—watching TV, playing computer games, surfing the Net, talking on the phone, shopping. This does not have to be a bad habit (just as eating is not a bad thing), but it's something you will choose to give up for a certain period of time so you can focus on God in a special way.

These suggestions are little more than an introduction to a large and incredible topic. But a journey has to begin somewhere.

Let's return to our overall topic of chronic tiredness because of too many losses in our spiritual battles with the enemy. What we need is a better way to match his fire power, a secret weapon that will even things up. With this in mind, let's quickly look at another remarkable story in Scripture.

In 2 Chronicles 20, the people of God are threatened by the Moabites, the Ammonites, and the Meunites. That's like having to wrestle Wood River, East St. Louis, and Granite City all on the same day!

Alarmed, King Jehoshaphat proclaimed a fast throughout the nation. As he prayed publicly, he said to God, "We have no power to face this vast army that is attacking us" (verse 12, NIV). Then the monarch referred to the same passage of Scripture Bill Bright wrote about, 2 Chronicles 7. Jehoshaphat reminded God how he was the one who told Judah to come to the temple when they were in trouble. There his people were to humble themselves, seek his face, and turn from their wicked ways. At such a time they would hear from heaven. That's precisely where the frightened men of Judah had gone with their wives and children.

Through Jahaziel the prophet, God told the nation that the battle wasn't theirs, but his. They were to march out to meet the enemy unafraid, because they wouldn't have to fight. Then the passage reveals that the invaders turned against one another and there was a great slaughter. When Jehoshaphat's troops arrived on the scene, they found nothing except dead bodies all over the place—plus so much plunder it took them three days to gather it all!

Would this victory have happened if the people had not fasted? I don't think so. And I don't believe the people of God will know victory today without resorting to fasting, either.

So the sooner we get started, the better. It's high time we rediscover a nearly forgotten weapon in the arsenal of the North American church. Beginning today, you can be one of the people of God who learns to use this grapevine clipper, this troop energizer, this incredibly powerful spiritual weapon, this unique method of freeing God to work as he wills—this untapped miracle.

CHAPTER SIX

UNTAPPED MIRACLE
6

TELLING OUR STORIES

TELLING STORIES
by Greg Asimakoupoulos

Once upon a long ago,
in a time before I knew that
happily ever after
would never be true
this side of Heaven,
the Caretaker of the Cosmos
created a person called "me."
And lest you think differently,
I'll admit it right off:
The person called "me"
isn't always the me
that you see.
I'm a fairy tale
trapped in real life.
May I share with you my story?
It's not a best-selling novel,
but it's true.
And when I'm through,
I'd like to hear the story that is yours.

Inertia is usually not a problem you want to be responsible for solving. Inertia means inactivity—even sluggishness. Someone who's sluggish is lacking in energy, indisposed to action, lazy.

Can you imagine a winning coach announcing, "We are ecstatic that our number-one pick in this year's draft was known all through college for his remarkable inertia"? Or an employer bestowing a promotion on the basis of some worker's consistent pattern of inertia? Or a parent boasting, "My daughter's inertia really pleases me"? Of course not!

I can still remember a cartoon I saw as a kid in grade school. It was one that came inside a penny Double Bubble Gum purchase. A kid was slouched at his desk half asleep. His teacher asked a simple math question and then had to wait and wait and wait for an answer. When the response finally came, she shook her ruler at the student and snapped, "Isn't there anything you can do fast?"

"Yes," was the reply. "I can get tired fast!" Maybe my recall is so keen because I showed the cartoon to my mother, who had zero tolerance for anyone not doing his or her best at all times. She saw no humor whatsoever in that comic.

I can confidently predict, then, that pastors looking for a new place to serve will not go for a congregation with a reputation for spiritual inertia. Resolving that kind of conundrum is a little like a minister trying single-handedly to move a drugged elephant from the church sanctuary to the fellowship hall. And yet inertia has become a rather commonplace problem in churches.

GUNG HO CHRISTIANS

What causes it? What puts troops at ease, making them inactive and inattentive when they're supposed to be up and at 'em? More than one contributing factor is usually involved. In fact, several have already been discussed in this book. But here's another nuance that needs to be addressed: Throughout the ranks of the church, we have far too few times when we share personal stories that reveal what's exciting about being Christian!

It's like soldiers, sailors, Marines, or Air Force pilots never talking about anything that's happened to them in the military—even with each other. With no such normal interaction going on, before long the top brass would have a major morale problem to deal with. Instead, they want gung ho people who not only talk, but practically eat, drink, and sleep national defense.

How gung ho is the average church person about his or her faith? My fear is, new believers quickly come to the conclusion that too much spiritual enthusiasm can get you in trouble—not only with non-Christians, but also with the average, long-standing church-member. That's because when you examine all the conversations that take place between church people, very few of them relate to critical issues regarding the faith. On occasion, the pastor's sermon might be discussed, but there's a better chance people will say what they liked or disliked about it, rather than how it affected their lives. A request for prayer is more likely to be a physical concern than a spiritual one. And if you overhear someone in an animated conversation about how to aggressively move forward the cause of Christ, you've probably stumbled by mistake into a conference on world missions.

Now, I know I'm painting with broad brush strokes. What I'm describing isn't always the case. In fact, just last week I had two experiences that fall outside this generalization—on opposite sides of the spectrum. The first came when I went out for an early breakfast. At the table next to mine two young men had their Bibles open. They were studying a passage of Scripture together and talking about how it relates to their day-to-day life. That was wonderful. Then, the very next day, a friend was telling me about the rural church his family was now attending. While trying to get to know people better, he discovered that after the service some of the men apparently made it a habit to meet behind the church to share dirty jokes!

Both these storytelling experiences are exceptions to the rule I'm measuring with, and my purpose is not to make things sound better or worse than they really are. Rather, I'm trying to describe as accurately as possible where the average church person is when it comes to talking about his or her faith.

TALKING THE WALK

With this in mind, I wouldn't accuse Christians of not walking their talk. The issue is more basic than that: few of them even talk about their walk! And with serious conversation about spiritual matters nearly missing from their lives, they're free to walk in whatever direction they want—certainly their infrequent words about their Christian faith have little chance of ever catching up with them. This creates a condition worse than spiritual fatigue. It's a Christian walk that's inert, at a complete standstill. And why would God's people change if they don't even recognize their condition, if they have nobody shaking a ruler at them and demanding, "What's the problem with you sluggards, anyway?"

Well, putting one's shoulder under the groggy elephant and giving a couple of mighty shoves may not be the best job around, but somebody's got to do it. So for this chapter, my bottom line reads: *Telling stories of God's wondrous involvement in our lives overcomes the inertia that develops when believers fail to recognize what he's doing.*

> **THE KEY: TELLING STORIES OF GOD'S WONDROUS INVOLVEMENT IN OUR LIVES OVERCOMES THE INERTIA THAT DEVELOPS WHEN BELIEVERS FAIL TO RECOGNIZE WHAT HE'S DOING.**

A slothlike manner marks church people when they aren't challenged to be on the lookout for God's activity in their daily lives. It's clear we have real problems if Christians seldom refer to the Lord's real presence as they converse with one another, not to mention when they're out in the world. What chance do they have to move forward in their Christian walk of faith when they can't even identify where they are right now? And how can they ask for help from others when they know nothing about the places fellow believers have traveled?

The secret solution? The miracle cure? Get folks to start telling stories of God's delightful involvement in their lives. And in every church, a certain few can prime the pump for others, bringing new energy not only to themselves, but eventually to the entire congregation.

WHERE STORIES ARE TOLD

Sharing stories of God's involvement in our lives can occasionally be done during the main worship service. I mention this first because many people only attend church on Sunday morning or Saturday night. Thinking about my own local congregation, I remember a number of occasions this past year when our pastor's sermon was right on target in terms of my needs. But what stands out most vividly in my memory is a five- or six-minute segment when a church member told about his experience with tithing.

What initially caught my attention is that this gentleman started by mentioning that he learned to tithe when he was young. That was my situation as well. When I was a young boy, my parents taught me to give the Lord 10 percent right off the top of all the money I earned. They considered that a minimum. I too had been well trained. But then this man testified that in his middle years he went through a highly traumatic financial situation. For a good while he didn't know whether or not his company would make it. There were occasions when he wasn't paid because there was just no money. By this time in his story I was listening with both ears, because again I knew only too well what that was like. But all during those tough times, whenever he was paid, this man continued to tithe. He said he wasn't quite sure why, but because everything else about his life was precarious he had no desire to be out of sorts with his Provider. Then he told how the Lord began to turn things around and that once again he's experiencing financial prosperity. I'm not at that place yet, but his story touched me deeply, in a way no biblical exposition on tithing ever had. What's interesting is that I had never really gone out of my way to meet this person. At that moment, however, I was aware that I could learn a great deal from him. And it fascinates me that as I look back on the church year this was the moment that stood out as being most memorable.

Would you agree that churches might benefit by occasionally scheduling times for laypeople to share in this way? I'm thinking about a church service where the main topic is a problem like peer pressure. Great Bible texts can be found to deal with such an issue. The first chapter of Daniel, for example, is about four young Hebrew men who were taken captive to far-off Babylon. There, rather than defile themselves with the rich food of the king's court, they put their lives on the line. Most church people will know the names of this fearsome foursome and what they did almost as soon as their minister brings up the passage. So don't look for any major surprises in the sermon.

But the congregation might find fascinating a contemporary peer-pressure tale. What about one from a junior high student who was pressured to do drugs and still said no? How about that advertising account executive who felt uneasy about a television commercial she was expected to produce? It seemed misleading, so she challenged the client. Will details of her go-against-the-flow story capture the interest of the congregation? I really think so! It might even be worth cutting a sermon short by a few minutes to free the necessary time for everyone to hear what happened. Would first-person stories like these detract from or add to a good message? You know the answer without even having to think about it, don't you?

Christian education classes and small group meetings are other obvious times for people to share accounts of how God is working in their lives. Leighton Ford uses the neat phrase "a collision of narratives" in his book *The Power of Story*. This is when God's story runs into your story. Leighton believes all Christians have encounters of this sort. In his words, "Each of us has a story—what I call 'a story with a small *s*,' the story of our own lives. At some point in our journey through life, our story collides with the Story of God—'the Story with a large *S*.' God's story calls our story into question. We must make a choice: either to reject the Story of God or to merge our story with His Story" (p. 10).

> IT'S ALMOST IMPOSSIBLE NOT TO LISTEN TO SOMEONE WHO BEGINS WHAT HE OR SHE HAS TO SAY WITH, "LET ME SHARE SOMETHING UNUSUAL THAT HAPPENED..."

Again, we live in a storytelling culture. Other church members might discount your opinion or disagree with your answer to a question about the meaning of a verse of Scripture, but they will be hard-pressed to dismiss your story. You see, it's almost impossible not to listen to someone who begins what he or she has to say with, "Let me share something unusual that happened...."

I've found I don't really know people until I've heard them tell a few of their "spiritual collision" stories. Then often I realize I've had the privilege of sitting next to someone quite special. I wanted to applaud when I heard a grandfather tell how he was the first person to the hospital when news came that one of his grandchildren had been in a serious accident. Taking the young man's hand, he prayed tearfully, and he knew by the way his hand had been squeezed that he had verbally walked this precious young man right into the presence of Jesus. What a privilege and joy it is to hear such accounts of God's involvement in our lives, even during our most difficult moments. And how wonderful for those who are sharing to have their experiences affirmed and applauded by their brothers and sisters in faith. On the other hand, I can't underscore enough how tragic it is when the people of the church for some reason stop telling their stories. Don't let this happen.

Sometimes church classes are structured to look a whole lot like mini worship services. The chairs are arranged in auditorium fashion and people do more listening than they do talking. This isn't necessarily bad, because a lot can be learned from a gifted teacher. But a major problem develops when there's too much feeding and not enough feedback, too much passivity and not enough participation. The way to spell the problem is I-N-E-R-T-I-A. The drugged elephant just gets heavier and heavier.

BIBLICAL STORYTELLING

I've always been impressed by the teaching style of Jesus. He was quick to get his disciples involved in what was going on. He spent time in debriefing sessions, making sure they were on top of things as much as possible. He invited their stories to collide with his.

This interactive learning style marked the early church as well. Meeting in homes and sharing meals in informal gatherings, these first church members talked together a great deal, I'm sure. And I doubt their conversations centered on the price of a new donkey or the recent changes in the weather! Certainly these early believers discussed the exciting things God was doing in their individual lives, in their communities, and in an ever-expanding world that was waking up to the incredible news that God had sent his Son to earth on a most remarkable mission. Those who had witnessed Christ's life, death, and resurrection firsthand must have talked about their observations and shared insights into what they'd seen. And as new believers came into the fold, they undoubtedly added to these eyewitness accounts with their own stories of faith.

This is not all that dissimilar to a method God himself used in the Old Testament. When necessary, he spoke directly with a leader like Moses. His conversations with Joshua, however, were not as frequent. That's because the Lord made sure Joshua had opportunity to watch the Moses story up close and personally.

"As I was with Moses, so I will be with you," God says in Joshua 1:15 (NIV). "I will never leave you nor forsake you." This promise had to be extremely meaningful, because Joshua knew exactly how God had been with his predecessor. The Moses story was one he understood almost as well as he did his own. In fact, Joshua had served as best supporting actor in that blockbuster escape movie!

DON'T BE AFRAID

The same kind of mentoring could happen in our day, if we would only begin sharing our faith experiences with others. And what an incredible energy infusion those stories could provide! Think of the young man or woman just entering the faith. This new believer wouldn't have to start from square one. He or she could jump ahead because of what's been shared by those more mature in their faith. And how wonderful for even the most seasoned warrior to enter a new "battlefield" of spiritual struggle armed with proven tactics perfected by others.

The ideal is that Christians could someday talk about where they are spiritually as easily as they discuss movies, sports, gardening, cars, or jobs. Some are able to do this. Most are more guarded. They pretend their walk with the Lord is something too personal to share. More likely, it's an area of insecurity for them. Afraid of opening a Pandora's box, they prefer things the way they are. *Safe* is what they would call it. My word is—you guessed it—*inert*. Webster defines *inert* as "tending to be mentally inactive, without power to move." I admit that while *safe* is a more attractive term, *inert* is probably more accurate.

Maybe this whole discussion has become more intimidating to you than it needs to be. Let me ask, are you learning to find tension's good side? That was Untapped Miracle #1. The process of working through a tough situation is actually a way your story and his Story are colliding. I can almost guarantee that hearing about your discovery of tension's good side will prove interesting to your Christian friends!

The To, Through, and Talk About game challenges you to be a 24/7 Christian—Untapped Miracle #2. Certainly it's not too personal to tell a fellow believer one way you feel God has ministered to you or through you on a given day. Can you see how these are also small, but meaningful occasions when the natural and the supernatural collide?

My wife, Karen, wrote that "a Christian home is a miracle to be shared." She didn't pen that line because she thinks followers of Christ are better decorators or chefs. Rather, the living Christ is often able to make his presence known in home settings where distractions have been kept at a minimum and the occasion of getting together has been covered by prayer. And when in our times together we recognize Jesus in our midst, conversations naturally flow regarding all the good things he has done for us. So again, there's a natural link between Christian hospitality—Untapped Miracle #3—and telling our stories of faith.

Letting your pastor know how a sermon impacted your life is another easy method of saying how your story and Christ's Story have come together. Suggesting a topic you would find helpful in the future makes a statement as well. You're saying, "There's a chapter of my life yet to be lived, and I'd like God's help. I need to learn how to take a direction different from the one in which I'm presently headed."

What's easier to talk about with a friend than a shared experience? That's another great reason to team up with someone and start learning about fasting— Untapped Miracle #5. Because it is an area you probably shouldn't tackle on your own, from its inception this new discipline in you life can be a shared story—not just by word of mouth, but by mutual experience.

None of these are intimidating suggestions. They don't demand that the first time you talk about spiritual matters you must reveal your very soul. On the other hand, you'll probably be amazed at what a jump-start these early efforts can be for your drained religious battery. Telling our stories—that's Untapped Miracle #6. It can even overcome the inertia that develops among believers who are habitually oblivious to what God is doing.

I know I'm nudging the elephant, and it might still be resisting. But listen—miracles require Christ's touch. That's a given. But more than once in the gospels, they also required some small faith steps on the part of the people wanting help.

STORYTELLING HOW-TO'S

Let me share a final thought with you as a potential church pump-primer. The way you tell your story is important. Don't try to impress others with how spiritual you are. The result will be the exact opposite of what you want. The more human you can make yourself, the better. And if possible, end your testimony with a question such as, "Have you ever had a similar experience?"

Let me illustrate. In a recent discussion about the conscience, I explained that sometimes it's like an alarm going off in my head. *"Bzzzzzzz!,"* it says, "Do this" or "Stop doing that." I use *Bzzzzzzz!* because I never hear actual words from the Lord. It's more like a persistent warning or an interruption that means, "Now hear this!"

At a recent small group gathering, I shared that I'm not always sure it's the Lord, but I try to give him the benefit of the doubt. For example, on a certain weekend I was scheduled to speak in Indiana. Traveling by car with my wife, I wanted to leave the Chicago area before the heavy Friday afternoon traffic set in. If we made it onto the expressway by mid-afternoon, we could skirt around the city and hopefully save an hour by avoiding the worst of the tie-ups. Unfortunately, I was running late, and before I could pick Karen up I needed to stop at the bank and also at the office to sign some letters.

I went to the drive-up window and wrote a check for cash. When it's a short weekend trip like this, I ask for different denominations of bills so I can divide them up over the three days. If I don't spend more than I've allotted for the first day, I should be all right for day two. If I can keep up the pattern, on the third day we have enough to stop for a nice meal on the way home.

I was counting the money in the envelope when I was interrupted by a voice over the drive-up intercom saying, "Reverend Mains, Reverend Mains! How are you?" I looked at the young man behind the glass in the bank and for the life of me couldn't figure out who it was. On top of that, he was interrupting my counting and the distraction was a little bit annoying. *Who is that, Lord?* I questioned as I answered, "I'm fine. How are you?"

"Well, I'm doing wonderfully well," was the response. "I'm getting married tomorrow!" If there's anything ministers should be good at, it's knowing who is getting married. So, this just added to my frustration.

"Who are you marrying?" I asked, hoping that he could hear me. (You're never sure whether or not they have the listening button pressed down.)

"Oh, I'm marrying Becky ————," he replied.

"Well, praise the Lord!" was my response. I knew her. She was a friend of my youngest son. Her folks were missionaries, and they were wonderful people. "I'm so glad for you," I continued. "The Lord be with you." And then, because cars were starting to line up behind me, I drove on.

> I KNOW MINISTERS ARE SUPPOSED TO BE ABLE TO TELL WHETHER OR NOT GOD HAS SPOKEN, BUT IN THIS SITUATION I HONESTLY DIDN'T KNOW.

Waiting for the traffic to go by so I could get out onto the main street and hurry to the office to sign my letters, a *Bzzzzzzz!* went off in my mind. *Maybe he's a missionary kid as well. He was so happy about getting married tomorrow. He recognized me; I didn't even know him. Maybe I should do something for him. I should probably give him $20 so he can go out for dinner with his new bride on their honeymoon.*

But if I do that, I'm going to be 20 bucks short on my first day and I haven't even started yet. On top of that I've got to get some gas and I'm running late. Was it you, Lord, *or did I think of this complication myself? I'll tell you what, Jesus. If I close my eyes and count to ten and there's not any traffic and I can pull out, I'll go back into the line and give the kid $20. If not, I'm beating it out of here, because I'm already late . . . 6, 7, 8, 9, 10.*

I opened my eyes and the street was as clear as if it had been 3:00 in the morning. Figuring I had witnessed no small miracle, I drove around and waited in line until I could get up to the teller window once again.

I know ministers are supposed to be able to tell whether or not God has spoken, but in this situation I honestly didn't know. As I waited in the line the second time, I was tempted to pull away and get over to the office and sign those letters, because this was taking a lot more time than it should have.

When it was finally my turn, I looked and I couldn't see the young man anywhere. I asked the new teller where the fellow was who was getting married tomorrow and, wouldn't you know it, he had taken a bathroom break!

Oh, I'll write him a note, I thought. But I didn't have a pencil. "Could you send a pencil out, please?" The bank didn't have a pencil, but it had a nice ball-point pen with their advertisement on the barrel. Unfortunately, they weren't as well-equipped with stationery. Finally, I had to write around the edges of an unused bank deposit slip.

It's very difficult to write a warm personal note to someone on a bank deposit slip when you don't even know his name! All of this began to seem very silly. So I just wrote, "You have a wonderful bride-to-be. Our family really likes Becky. . . ." I couldn't figure out if Becky spelled her name with a *cky* or a *cci. Well, I'll just take a poke at it, and if I misspell it, he'll have to excuse me.* "Here's $20. Enjoy a meal on us during your honeymoon. Say hi to her parents for me."

I put the $20 with the note and sent it through the machine. I wished I could re-copy it, because I'd crossed out several words. In fact, it looked a little bit like a note from a junior high friend who'd wanted to do something nice but wasn't very adept at it. Now I was once again waiting at the street for the traffic to clear, inwardly grousing about the Lord always seeming so vague when he talks to me.

About three minutes later I was at the office. I had purposely come in the side door so no one would see me. I needed to get my sermon notes, sign the letters, and then be on my way home. At the same time I had to figure out how to tactfully explain to Karen why I was so much later than I'd said I'd be. As soon as I sat at the desk there was another definite *Bzzzzzzz!* It wasn't the Holy Spirit, however. This was much louder. It was my secretary on the intercom. "There's someone here to see you," she said.

Thanks a lot, Lord. Did I forget an appointment? That's not characteristic of me. I'm in such a hurry. What could this be? I thought we were a team. Somehow we're going to have to learn to work together better.

"There's a gentleman here to see you," I was told. "He knows he doesn't have an appointment. He says you've helped him many times, and he just wants a minute."

Usually people who just want a minute have a two-hour problem to share. I told my secretary I didn't want to be rude, but I'd have to keep signing my letters while we talked. Then I'd have to leave because I was speaking in Indiana. Could she try to make that sound as important as possible?

A moment later the door opened and there was the gentleman. I recognized him immediately, and it was true, at a difficult time in his life, I had played a supportive role.

"I wasn't sure whether or not I'd be able to see you," he said. "So I wrote a note." (I wondered, fleetingly, if he had used a bank deposit slip.) "I know you're in a hurry," he continued, "so just read it when you can." Then he dropped it on the desk and he was on his way.

Wow! That was fast. Not bad, Lord. Scratch the comment about us not working together as well as I'd like.

I put the envelope in my coat pocket and finished signing the letters. Rather than risk going through the office where there might be additional interruptions, I buzzed my secretary and said I was on my way, adding, "Thanks for being a good defensive lineman!"

It's about a six-minute drive from the office to my home. About two minutes into the route I remembered the letter in my coat pocket. I know you're not supposed to read while you're driving, but I was curious as to what he'd written. Sometimes kind words are like a tonic to a minister, and heaven knows I needed some balm to soothe my racing spirit. I opened the envelope. There was no letter; all that was inside was a $50 bill. I was amazed. Chuckling, my first thought was: *Lord, if I'd known this was going to happen, I would have given the kid 40 bucks—then I would probably have ended up with 100!*

I know that's not the most spiritual response a minister could have. But isn't it interesting? There was an immediate connection in my mind between the earlier arguable prompting of the Holy Spirit and this affirmation from God not much later. Instead of being financially behind on my first day, I felt as wealthy as a king! And if I went the full speed limit, and hit some of the lights just right, I wouldn't have too much trouble beating most of the traffic.

As I shared the experience with the group, I added a question at the end. "Have any of you had an experience like this?" The response was almost immediate. In fact, most of the people in my small group could identify, and we spent a delightful 45 minutes hearing one individual after

> I HAD PRIMED THE PUMP BY BEING VULNERABLE. I DIDN'T TRY TO MAKE MYSELF APPEAR LIKE A CANDIDATE FOR PROTESTANT SAINT OF THE MONTH.

another share similar situations they'd experienced. When it was all over, we were thoroughly convinced God does speak to us—sometimes more clearly than others, but the interchange is definitely there. All of us agreed we need to improve in our listening, but there was also a sense of delight with the personal encounters with the supernatural that had obviously been going on.

I had primed the pump by being vulnerable. I didn't try to make myself appear like a candidate for Protestant Saint of the Month. And I had also asked a question that allowed others to share. Quite frankly, I was amazed by how they immediately built on my story, piping in with experiences of their own.

I shouldn't have been surprised. Over the years I have learned that when it comes to pump-priming, a good question is often as effective as a good story. Together, they're a powerful one-two punch:

◆ What is on the cutting edge for you spiritually right now?

◆ What lesson has God recently taught you?

◆ Can you talk about an individual who has challenged you to a deeper walk with the Lord?

◆ If you could relive a spiritual experience, what's one you would choose?

◆ Is there something you want the Lord to do through your life before you pass on?

Questions help others talk about their faith. It probably doesn't need to be said, but it's also important to listen closely to how people answer and draw them out even more. But remember the bottom line: As your fellow believers learn to talk about God's delightful involvement in their lives, it's going to help overcome the huge problem of inertia the church has struggled with for years.

Looking for more hints? Here are some steps you can take toward this energizing miracle:

◆ Be on the lookout for different settings in which people can hear the ways God has shown himself in the lives of others.

◆ For idea starters on telling your own stories, use

the lessons you've learned throughout this book.

◆ When sharing a story, don't be afraid to let your humanity show.

◆ To further prime the pump, ask good questions. (I've coauthored a book that can help: *Getting Beyond "How Are You?"* Look for information at the end of this publication.)

These may seem like simple steps to overcome the huge problem of inertia. But I dare you to try putting the miracle of telling your stories into practice. Listen! You just might hear an elephant trumpeting next time you drive by the church.

CHAPTER SEVEN

UNTAPPED MIRACLE

7

THE WIDER KINGSHIP

THE KING'S SHIP

by Greg Asimakoupoulos

> The King's Ship
> waits to weigh anchor,
> even though the winds of revival
> have begun to blow
> and the time to sail has come.
> The Captain appears willing
> to wait at the pier
> for a brief while more
> to give his passengers time
> to unpack their belongings
> and leave their baggage below
> and to gather as one
> on the deck.

When I was younger and less seasoned, I volunteered to be part of a three-man piano moving team. A friend asked if I could help relocate his baby grand. I had never done a job like this before, but I was still in my twenties, strong, and feeling pretty capable. The truth is, I wasn't experienced enough to say, "Forget it!"

This beautiful, black, but unwieldy beast was kept in a practice studio. The owner wanted it coaxed across town to his second floor apartment. I'm just glad we did the job before the "baby" was full grown.

A piano has wheels so it can easily be pushed across a room. But to be maneuvered through a doorway, the instrument needs to be tipped vertically. It was during this process that I first realized how heavy these monsters are. I had earlier moved large dressers and big stoves and heavy refrigerators—but this piano was in a sumo class all its own.

With great effort, the three of us finally completed the task of getting it out of the studio and strapped onto a rented trailer. I thought sawing it in half right at middle C would have made the task much easier, but that idea was nixed.

When the three of us arrived at the new location, the stairway didn't look all that imposing. Little did I know moving that baby grand piano up just one flight of stairs would make the apartment seem like it was perched at the top of the Washington Monument. And how could this beautiful instrument, capable of making such soft and gentle music, suddenly become a ponderous, lethal mass ready to crush us at the first opportunity with no twinge of conscience whatsoever?

All I could think of was an episode on the old *Candid Camera* television show, in which a beautiful woman in heels and a fancy outfit carries an obviously heavy suitcase down a city sidewalk. With a sigh, she sets it down over a metal grating. Because she's so attractive, it's only a moment before several strangers come up and spontaneously ask if they can help. "Oh, thank you," she says, smiling. "I just need to take this to the hotel entrance down the street." Pointing to where she's headed, she remarks in very feminine tones, "I *am* rather exhausted." In the meanwhile, the *Candid Camera* crew has secretly turned on a powerful electromagnet. The suitcase is now locked to the grating, making it all but impossible to lift.

Next the hidden camera captures what's designed to delight the television audience. Strong men strain and groan and sweat and make excuses and say bad words that were later bleeped out. But they can't budge this piece of luggage. Finally, the woman tells her would-be helpers, "Thank you. You have all been most gallant. Believe me, after carrying it for three blocks, I know how heavy this suitcase is." The electromagnet is switched off by the hidden crew. She grabs the handle, picks up the case, and struggles on her way. And the expressions of wonderment on the faces of the Sylvester Stallone-type men left standing there are just what the producer had in mind when he came up with this dynamite idea.

Unfortunately, my personal stairway-to-the-stars piano experience also felt like an electromagnet had been turned on. But no guy came popping out to say, "Smile, you're on *Candid Camera*." So the three of us, obviously needing more helping hands, or at least some lift training, grudgingly went about completing our obligation. Looking back, we were lucky the shiny instrument didn't fall back on us and snuff out our lives in early manhood.

I remember later being so exhausted and sore that

I could hardly muster the strength to climb into bed and drop off to sleep. Decades have passed, but I still recall with incredible detail that bone-tired feeling. And ever since then I have known how to respond whenever the first hint is dropped about moving someone's piano!

BONE-TIRED BELIEVERS

Because I recognize the evasion technique, I've realized that more and more Christians react this same way when asked to help with a job of any magnitude at the church. They've become too smart to casually agree, "Sure you can nominate my name for the board," or "Yes, count on me helping you out with the youth group," or "We can take in the missionary family for a month. No problem."

That's because they're tired—sometimes bone-tired. Church people have learned from experience how much work it is to teach a Christian education class every week, especially when their own Bible knowledge is limited and there's no one to call the evening before if they need help. They know how hard it is to prepare the meal for the annual mother-daughter banquet and also line up an adequate musician or speaker and decorate the entire gym with the help of only a skeleton crew. And they remember what it's like to find enough teachers and a music leader for Vacation Bible School, only to discover that the church down the street has chosen the same week and is planning a fun-fair complete with a balloon launch. So church people today are not going to offer to pick up those daunting suitcases anymore— even if the new C. E. director takes on a tired and help- less look and is one of the sharpest staff members ever hired by the church.

"Now pastor," they say when the minister stops by, "the family works hard. Can't add anything to the schedule right now. Need two incomes, you know. Free time isn't available like it once was. Besides, we've put in our time. Ten years ago we were part of a small church-planting team. Didn't even have an old upright to move into that rented facility. Sang with an accordion—sure did. But talk about work! Every Sunday and every other day we were at it. Went to bed exhausted. This was a new suburb back then. Had almost 10,000 people, and not a Christian witness anywhere until we started Grace Sanctuary. Had a seminary student as a part-time minister. He was as green as they come. He preached, but that's about all. The rest of us, just a handful, we did all the pastor-type stuff. Now that was a heavy load—especially with so few of us and no one to go to for help or advice. What did you say?"

> "WHEN I SAID THERE WEREN'T ANY OTHER CHURCHES, I MEANT BIBLE-BELIEVING CHURCHES. ONES THAT THINK LIKE WE DO. YOU UNDERSTAND, DON'T YOU?"

"I asked, wasn't there another church of any kind?"

"Well the Catholics had a big thing going. They're always early out of the blocks. Now that I think about it, there may have been a couple of Catholic churches."

"And no other Protestant ones?"

"I believe there was an Assembly of God work going

pretty well. But they're Pentecostal, you know. And some kind of Lutherans had a church. New building. Ever notice Lutherans always build attractive church buildings? Too bad they don't know Jesus."

"They don't, huh? Anyway, that's four other churches. What about Baptists?"

"Yeah, but mainliners, and who knows about them? Same way with the Methodists—although there was a kind of off-shoot Methodist group meeting in one of the grade schools. Then once I saw a minister with a long gray beard and a black robe at the grocery. He talked to the clerk at the check out counter like he knew her. Looked too fancy for a Roman Catholic, although she called him Father-something. But when I said there weren't any other churches, I meant Bible-believing churches. Ones that think like we do. You understand, don't you?"

Oh boy!

AVOIDING SPIRITUAL HERNIAS

Forgive me for being blunt, but when anyone talks this way, it strikes me as being like dumb Diotrephes. He's the man mentioned briefly in John's third epistle who refused to have anything to do with the beloved apostle. Actually, he wasn't open to any of the traveling brothers and sisters, and he spoke against those in his church who extended Christian hospitality them. His people were apparently the only real believers. Unfortunately, it wasn't God's truth Diotrephes had a corner on; it was just his own.

When we start believing that the future of Christianity rests on our church's efforts, and ours alone, I believe the devil just watches and laughs. He knows we're only going to get a spiritual hernia trying to lift his trick suitcase exclusively on our own! A number of Christians working together might be able to out-muscle his electromagnet, but this approach isn't often tried.

Sure, that other dad you met at the Boy Scout meeting said he'd graduated from Bible college. But he attends that ultraconservative church. I doubt his narrow insights on the Sunday school lesson you're preparing would be of help to your kids. *(Try a little bit harder; I'm sure you can lift it on your own.)*

It would be wonderful to invite all the kids from the housing project to your Vacation Bible School, but you don't really have the manpower to make it an outreach project, do you? That new congregation meeting in the grade school? Of course they have the people to help, and no facility for their VBS during the week. But the curriculum they use is a little old-fashioned. You'd have to compromise on the theme for the week. Maybe next year you can work something out. *(You say you hurt your back? Oh, that's too bad!)*

THE WIDER KINGSHIP

For hundreds of years Christians have concentrated on how they're *different.* I'd like to suggest that in the twenty-first century churches learn to concentrate more on how they are *alike.* Of course, in using this approach we'll still need to define who truly loves Jesus and who doesn't. No doubt there are some church groups that don't, or at least some who make our Lord less than what he is—

the unique Son of God. But when the troops are tired and there's only a handful of people to do a job that's too big to begin with, here's an important truth to get a handle on: *Isolated and exhausted congregations should consider the benefits of networking with the wider kingship.*

The word *kingdom* in Scripture can also be translated "kingship." I prefer that rendering. It makes sense to more people. When I refer to the kingship Christ established when he came to earth, it's made up of all those who bow their knee before him as their Lord and Savior. Christ's kingship has past, present, and future ramifications. Some Baptists honor his kingship by the way they live, and some don't. The same is true of Methodists, Lutherans, Pentecostals, and even non-Protestants—Catholics and Orthodox. Would you believe there are Salvation Army people who don't honor the King the way they should? That's true of Presbyterians, Mennonites, and Bible Church people as well. Of course, there are also many who do honor him.

> **THE KEY:**
> **ISOLATED AND EXHAUSTED CONGREGATIONS SHOULD CONSIDER THE BENEFITS OF NETWORKING WITH THE WIDER KINGSHIP.**

See, it's not all that easy to categorize Christians. If we write off all the Anglicans, we lose a marvelous author and Bible teacher like John R. W. Stott. If we close our minds to the Nazarenes, we eliminate family advocate Jim Dobson. If we can't stand Charismatics, we shut ourselves off to the largest television ministry in the country—Pat Robertson and the 700 Club. If we think all

Episcopalians are hopeless, to be consistent we should stop listening to Elizabeth Elliot's radio program.

In reality, Christians have made huge progress in overcoming earlier biases. Because of religious radio, we listen with open minds to Tony Evans or Chuck Swindoll, Woodrow Kroll or Steve Brown, and we're not always sure which one's into reformed theology and who's the president of Dallas Theological Seminary. Go into a Christian bookstore, and the variety of church backgrounds among the authors is mind-boggling. No one seems to see the need to unscramble the huge religious publishing egg that got mixed up years ago. But somehow, when it comes to local churches, we still hesitate about communicating outside our own walls. For non-Christians in our communities, this is one of the most befuddling of puzzles. Why can't Christians work together?

Fortunately, it's not necessary to come to a final conclusion on which churches are "kosher" and which ones aren't in order to network better. In fact, it's pretty hard to make an accurate assessment until we've started reaching out a little more. And once we do, instead of feeling the exhaustion of walking this road of faith alone, I'm pretty sure we'll begin to realize we're not as puny as we thought we were.

WORKING TOGETHER

In any given month, well over *half* the people in our country go to church or synagogue at least once. The number of those who are faithful in their worship attendance every week hovers around the 45 percent mark. What an incredible figure! Seeing it on paper doesn't impress us all that much. But participating in a huge Promise Keepers rally can sure bring this truth to life. The experience of sixty or seventy thousand men in a giant stadium all singing the praises of Jesus reduces many to tears. It may be just the sound, but some of what's happening is that these PK-ers are realizing what Christian women found out years before when they started holding their large conventions: As Christians we're not really alone. What transpires on the Lord's Day involves a lot more than the hundred or so people who sit in the pews at our own church.

If it's tiring to feel isolated, it's exhilarating to suddenly realize you're a part of something that's bigger than you ever dreamed. That's why every time a viable interchurch effort is organized, it's a good idea for ministers to promote it. The annual March For Jesus involves millions of Christians worldwide. Yet on a local level, someone's eyes are always popping at the sight of a friend he or she never thought of as a fellow follower of Christ. Protestants and Catholics have benefited in more ways than one from working together in the pro-life movement. And having participated in them myself, I pity the congregation that opts to ignore community days of prayer or joint Christian efforts to reach out to the poor.

To keep the reality of the greater kingship in my own mind, I have found it helpful to occasionally go to more than one church on a Sunday morning. Because multiple services are often held, it's possible to attend at 8:00 A.M. at my own church and somewhere else at 10:00 A.M. (Admittedly, I haven't done this as often since we started hosting after-church brunches.) Going to other churches gives me an opportunity to meet people I don't usually come in contact with, but who nevertheless love Jesus just like I do. If I visit an African-American congregation or one that's Asian or Hispanic, the style of worship isn't always what I'm accustomed to. But it's still a positive experience, and my prejudices sometimes need to be challenged.

When the troops are tired, it's important to think seriously about this issue of the wider kingship. That's because I believe something unusual is happening in our land, something that would be the greatest re-energizer the church in North America could possibly experience.

KINGDOM RENEWAL

I feel certain that the Lord is carefully preparing his people for another full season of revival. The word *revival* means literally "life coming back again." If a healthy person faints, you hope he or she can be revived and quickly return to the best of health. The same is true of the church. And looking back at times of renewal described in Scripture and recorded throughout history, these unusual seasons of spiritual vitality are always marked by an overwhelming sense of the presence of the Lord. It's almost as though Jesus himself bodily participates in the life of his church for an extended period of time. That's an energizer! But it also takes a while for the stage to be set.

Picture what would happen in your congregation if the King of kings came, and your people could see him not just through eyes of faith, but with their normal vision. Recognizing him, many would drop to their knees in worship.

The word *worship* means "to attribute worth to God." In the last few decades, the Lord has given his church a marvelous new understanding of what it means to worship him. Many congregations of every denomination now think nothing of spending twenty minutes or more in pure praise. I believe this is one of the ways the Lord has been preparing his people for a season of glorious revival.

When the presence of Jesus is experienced by his people, they begin to love each other. He demands it! On the denominational level, I see considerable progress being made here. On the local scene, however, it seems like it's harder to bring down the high walls. Churches in too many communities are separated by suspicion and jealousy, and racial barriers haven't been eliminated to the degree they should be. But we're further along than we were 20 years ago. Why? Because God is doing a great work among Christians who need to be more loving toward those in other congregations.

A burst of Christian service is also evident during times of revival. When people clearly see their King, they realize he's done far more for them than they have for him, and consequently, they look for ways to serve. When I first began in ministry, very little was said about spiritual gifts. Now it's hard to find a churchgoer who hasn't read something on the topic. Many people can identify their primary spiritual gifts, and Christians have learned a great deal about this subject from the experiences of those in other churches. If the Lord blesses us with another outpouring of his Spirit, I believe his people will be prepared to use their gifts to reach out and serve the world in a phenomenal way!

Revival and prayer have always been inseparable. Why? When people recognize Jesus' presence, they want to talk to him. Have you noticed how the current prayer movement continues to build? The momentum is incredible, and it hasn't crested yet. Couple that with the recent "reawakening" across denominational lines regarding the power of fasting. These early stages of revival are exciting as you watch them start to unfold! But that disclosure is happening precisely because people are beginning to reach across their various Christian divisions to seek together the one true God.

Authentic revival always results in evangelism. For a long time it seemed like churches in North America had forgotten how to reproduce. Now a powerful new influence called the "seeker church movement" has been raised up. Whether or not you attend such a congregation, you'll have to agree that they have caused pastors and congregations of every persuasion to consider anew the matter of evangelism. Praise the Lord! Christ came to seek and to save the lost. When his influence marks churches, evangelism will be front and center.

Next, when Christ makes his presence known, it's not long before the enemy also shows up in force. Frank Peretti's popular book *This Present Darkness* pointed out this principle. It was a timely work that forced readers to think in terms of the bigger picture of light versus darkness. It also spawned numerous other similar publications, and consequently, spiritual warfare has become a growing matter of concern for many churches. Pastors don't want their people to focus on the enemy, but they also don't want them to be ignorant of his wiles.

Finally, when revival comes, it becomes obvious that the church offers people the best life possible. When Christ is at the head, fully influencing all his people in the way he intends, it is indeed a privilege to be part of the body.

But how can we experience a sense of well-being when our families are manifesting all the same dysfunctions as the rest of society? I believe God is working on this problem. In recent years he's raised up numbers of gifted Christian counselors from various denominational backgrounds. They are well-trained and have a love for what the Scriptures teach. When the Spirit begins to work powerfully, hurting people will need more than sermons—there will have to be proper, one-on-one help. So one way to take advantage of the wider kingship is to get in touch with some of these professional and volunteer counselors scattered throughout Christendom. These people are already doing a great job, and I am sure the time is soon coming when their services will be in far greater demand.

> ONE WAY TO TAKE ADVANTAGE OF THE WIDER KINGSHIP IS TO GET IN TOUCH WITH SOME OF THESE COUNSELORS SCATTERED THROUGHOUT CHRISTENDOM.

These are just some of the characteristics that show up when God brings revival to his people. He has stacked the revival kindling quite high already, and hopefully, a divine match will soon be set to the pile. One matter troubles me, however. Local congregations haven't learned to work together nearly as well as they should. And if renewal sweeps in full, it won't make that problem any easier to solve. In fact, it could actually hinder what God is wanting to do.

Revival is a marvelous blessing, but it's also an incredibly chaotic time. Picture everyone moving church pianos up and down a stairway, all at the same time, at double speed. That's revival! When praying for revival, the great London pulpiteer Charles Spurgeon said, "God, send us a season of glorious disorder." He knew revival wouldn't be all peace and tranquillity.

Would you believe that more church splits occur during revival than at any other time? Don't let that throw you off. Times of revival also bring more church growth, more Christians going into full-time service, higher giving, and more conversions. So the picture is primarily good. But some people mistakenly see revival as an era of perfection, which it certainly isn't. So right now, before the momentum becomes almost more than we can handle, shouldn't churches become more cooperative and less competitive?

If you study accounts of past revivals, you'll discover they never happen in just one denomination at a time. Major movements of the Holy Spirit jump across many different Christian groups. For perspective, here's a short account from *Revival Times in North America,* by Fred W. Hoffman, about what took place during the frontier revivals in the early 1800s:

> Rev. B. W. Stone ... relates: "A memorable meeting was held at Cane Ridge in August, 1801. The

roads were crowded with wagons, carriages, horses and footmen moving to the solemn camp. It was judged that between twenty and thirty thousand persons were assembled. Four or five preachers spoke at the same time in different parts of the encampment without confusion. The Methodist and Baptist preachers aided in the work, and all appeared cordially united in it. They were of one mind and soul. The salvation of sinners was the one object. We all engaged in singing the same songs, all united in prayer, all preached the same gospel. The numbers converted will be known only in eternity. Many things transpired in the meeting which were so much like miracles that they had the same effect as miracles on unbelievers. By them many were convinced that Jesus was the Christ, and were persuaded to submit to Him. This meeting continued six or seven days and nights, and would have continued longer, but food for such a multitude failed. To this meeting many had come from Ohio and other distant parts. These returned home and diffused the same spirit in their respective neighborhoods, and similar results followed. So low had

> THEY WERE OF ONE MIND AND SOUL. THE SALVATION OF SINNERS WAS THE ONE OBJECT. ALL UNITED IN PRAYER, ALL PREACHED THE SAME GOSPEL.

religion sunk, and such carelessness had universally prevailed, I had thought that nothing common could have arrested and held the attention of the people." But God was at work in sovereign grace in these days, turning the hearts of men from ungodliness and iniquity unto Himself. (pages 76–77)

It's time to get in mind the bigger picture of what might happen in the near future. Widespread, genuine spiritual renewal is what thousands have been praying for. If our requests are sincere, it's time to begin thinking about greater cooperation between Christ-honoring churches.

GETTING STARTED

How could this begin to happen? I have sometimes been in church services where pastors pray for other congregations in town. This has always impressed me, and it is a pattern that could be easily copied. It would also be interesting from a historic vantage point to set up tours of various church buildings in a community. Seeing assorted sanctuaries for the first time and hearing the testimony of what God has done through these ministries would be a great encouragement to those from diverse congregations.

Will cooperation always prove a blessing? No one can guarantee that. I'm reminded of the old story about several small-town churches that got together to put on an Easter musical. On the evening of the performance, as the combined choir processed in, the high-heel of one of the altos stuck in the metal grating of the heating vent on the sanctuary floor. This fast-thinking Methodist woman didn't miss a step. She just slipped her foot out of the shoe and walked on, trying not to hobble and hoping no one would notice her bare foot under her long choir robe. The tenor who followed was a Presbyterian. Without missing a stride, he bent over and picked up the shoe, intending to secretly hand it to her later. Unfortunately, what he ended up with was not only the shoe, but also the grating in which it was tightly wedged. It was the well-trained Lutheran bass who got the worst end of the deal. Deeply engrossed in the music and failing to notice what was happening, he stepped right into the hole!

But we can't let minor failures stop us. I believe God is doing something wonderful and new in our day. In response, the enemy is anxiously working on his counterstrategy. "Don't abandon what's always worked for us," he tells his minions. "The pick-up-the-suitcase-by-yourself trick has seldom failed. Let's go for it again."

But this time, let Satan be the embarrassed one as our spiritual "candid camera" crew swings into operation. Instead of representatives from the various churches each trying to pick up this trick suitcase on their own, envision them surrounding it. Now see them wisely working together. As one, they reach down and grab hold of the metal grating, each hand at a strategic point that will give them a well-balanced overall power. With a great heave, they lift the suitcase, the grating, and the electromagnet all at the same time and carry it off, singing joyously:

We share our mutual woes,
Our mutual burdens bear;
And often for each other flows
The sympathizing tear.
Blest be the tie that binds
Our hearts in Christian love;
The fellowship of kindred minds
Is like to that above!

With everything working as planned, the enemy becomes quite agitated. Not thinking clearly, he runs after the strong men and women yelling, "You're not doing it right. It's supposed to be only one at a time. Come back!" Forgetting about the hole, perhaps he'll fall in, putting himself out of commission for a considerable while. And what a shame, from his perspective! This is the very time the work of the Lord starts to move forward full tilt!

What do you think? Isn't your congregation tired of tugging on that suitcase alone, getting tired, and feeling sillier by the minute? Even a partial fulfillment of this God-given dream is ample reason to consider the benefits of networking with believers from other Christian perspectives. And after a season of cooperating more, formerly isolated and exhausted congregations won't return to their earlier patterns until years down the road. That would have to be in the far distant future—after every last one who remembers the great joy of beating the enemy at his own game has gone home to be with the Lord.

CHAPTER EIGHT

UNTAPPED MIRACLE

8

THE LIVING CHRIST

WHEN THE TROOPS ARE TIRED

by Greg Asimakoupoulos

When the troops are tired,
and hope is gone,
and it seems we've lost the war,
the score is all but settled.
Our dreams and plans lie dying,
defeated by our foe.
But no!
Wait!
Don't raise the white flag yet.
Support has just arrived.
All bets are off!
Against all odds,
our mortally wounded
Commander-in-chief,
once dead,
is now alive.

There's a fast-food establishment half a mile from my office. It's on the southwest corner of a major intersection. The four east-west lanes are usually heavy with traffic, as are the four heading north and south. From all appearances, this franchise should be doing an incredible business. It's not, though.

The problem is, only hungry motorists going east can make an exit to purchase something. If you're westbound, it's practically impossible to turn into the restaurant—unless you want to jump a median and dart through two lanes of fast-moving cars and trucks. The same is true if you're headed north or south.

I happen to travel east on my way to work, so the drive-through is a convenient place for me to pick up a cup of coffee. I rarely find more than one car in front of me. Most of the time, I'm their only customer. Even so, it takes longer to get what I want there than it would if I stopped at a much busier place a little closer to the office.

Because business is slow due to the street arrangement, it appears the management has also cut back on employees. The same woman always asks over the intercom, "How can I help you?" then responds to my request for coffee and one cream with, "Would you like a cinnamon roll to go along with that?"

"No," I say, "just the coffee and cream." Then I drive to the window and wait. Then I wait some more. As far as I can tell, this lady is also tending the grill, taking care of walk-in customers, and working the cash register. So I sit in my car a good while before I finally get my coffee. As I do, I remind myself again to only stop here when I have lots of time, which most people—including me—don't have at 7:30 in the morning.

For this restaurant, it seems one problem has led to another. I predict that pretty soon they'll have to close down. Or else they will need to come up with some clever way to make "slow food" as attractive as fast food. With so many people whizzing by, it's too bad their enterprise is located in such a disadvantaged position.

It may just be my imagination, but I think you pick up a different demeanor from people who work at a struggling business, compared to a successful one. I know that's true of many churches. Visit one that's on a growth curve, and you can almost feel energetic life in the atmosphere. Attend a church that's not going any-where, and the air at the top of the sanctuary seems to hang heavy.

Would you believe, quite often the problem of tapped-out Christians and tired churches is one of posi-tioning? I'm not referring to the location of the church facility on a given block. Most church buildings are strategically situated, and I've visited lots of growing churches located far from the main thoroughfares of their town. The placement I have in mind relates to stay-ing close to the Living Christ as he pursues his mission of bringing all things in heaven and on earth under his rule (Ephesians 1:10). Let me unfold what that means. Of all the untapped miracles in this book, I've purpose-ly saved the best for last.

IN THE BEGINNING

Scripture teaches that Jesus created the world. The apos-tle John put it this way: "Through him [Christ] all things were made; without him nothing was made that has been made" (John 1:3). The incredible flowers my wife so enjoys tending are his handiwork far more than hers.

The marvelous variety of zoo animals I ooh and aah over with my grandchildren are a result of his creative genius. Then there's the awesome panorama of mountain ranges, which takes my breath away. I'm convinced Jesus is ultimately responsible for all this natural beauty.

The writer of Hebrews reveals that through Christ, God also made the universe (Hebrews 1:2). The splendor of the night skies is a demonstration of his remarkable skills. Are you aware that there are more heavenly bodies the size of our earth or larger than there are grains of sand upon the face of the earth? "For by him all things were created: things in heaven and on earth," echoes Paul writing about Jesus in Colossians 1:16, (NIV).

> WE'VE ALL HEARD ABOUT THE FALL. BUT "FALL" HAS LITTLE MEANING IF WE'RE NOT TOLD WHAT WE FELL FROM.

Human beings were designed to be at the apex of Christ's creative plan. We are amazing creatures. Hardly the result of mere time and chance, we were fashioned with great care by one who breathed into us his breath of life. And what did he say? I ask because too many believers have the impression that humankind was flawed from the beginning. Not so! The Maker declared enthusiastically on the sixth day of his creation project that his work was not only good, but very good.

The place where everything first came together, where there was so much love and such marvelous potential, was called Eden. It was a combination arboretum, orchard, farm, flower garden, zoo, and outdoor chapel. Here Adam and Eve enjoyed regular times of communing with their Lord. Were it not for the deceiver, that experience could still be enjoyed by people like my wife and grandchildren, or for that mater, any of us.

We've all heard about the Fall. But "fall" has little meaning if we're not told what we fell from. You can fall over your feet, off a stool, down a ladder, from a high-rise window, or out of a plane miles above the earth. The fall preachers talk about was a huge drop.

The first man and woman lost so much when they decided to listen to Satan. Genesis 3:8–11, 23–24 reads:

> Toward evening they heard the Lord God walking about in the garden, so they hid themselves among the trees. The Lord God called to Adam, "Where are you?"
>
> He replied, "I heard you, so I hid. I was afraid because I was naked."
>
> "Who told you that you were naked," the Lord God asked. "Have you eaten the fruit I commanded you not to eat?" So the Lord God banished Adam and his wife from the Garden of Eden, and he sent Adam out to cultivate the ground from which he had been made. After banishing them from the garden, the Lord God stationed mighty angelic beings to the east of Eden. And a flaming sword flashed back and forth, guarding the way to the tree of life.

Except for one glorious truth, it would have been hopeless to harbor thoughts of ever being elevated to our former high status. But for some inexplicable reason, God still cared deeply about all he had made. Because of this, he committed himself to doing everything in his power to restore this beautiful world to his original design. This included fixing the problem of people who have been broken by the Fall. To question why the Creator didn't act more quickly is to fail to appreciate the magnitude of what his plan involved and the great personal cost required to pull it off.

CHRIST THE KING

The word *reconciliation* means "to bring together warring parties." Paul wrote in 2 Corinthians 5 that God came to earth in the person of his Son to reconcile the world to himself. He was here to make peace with those who had aligned themselves with the enemy and also to eventually bring everything concerning creation back under his gracious rule.

Our thinking is truncated if we only see Christ's mission as one of rescuing individuals and preparing them for heaven. Certainly that's a key part of his overall purpose. But he also came to show us what a magnificent place this world was intended to be. The one who fashioned it would now model the designer style of loving God and loving people.

When he preached about his kingship, it was obviously good news for the poor. That's because this "new king on the block" truly cared about the problems of people with little power. The brokenhearted and any who mourned would find hope under his scepter. Those who hungered for righteousness would see it modeled before their very eyes and also have the chance to experience it personally. Justice and equity would be elevated under his rule along with mercy. Where? In all settings where the King was loved and his rule honored. That's what he was offering with his now and future kingdom, or kingship.

Observe how he lived when he was among us. Jaws dropped when onlookers took note of what he was doing. He seemed to change all the rules. No wonder the little people rejoiced! The lame and the blind and the outcasts found both a hearing and a healing with this young monarch. He was truly remarkable. Many were ready to position him on a Jewish throne. He refused, even as he continued teaching his subjects his world-changing ways.

Those who found Christ's ideas threatening sought to kill him. They didn't know they were playing into his hands. He understood this to be part of his mission. He knew what they didn't. A king's ransom had to be paid for sin. So he submitted to their wishes and went to the cross.

But he would rise again! This was imperative. He must defeat all enemies that held the world captive—not just Satan, but sin and death as well. Then everything would be put under Christ's feet, so he could in turn present everything to his Father (1 Corinthians 15:25).

Paul wrote, "If Christ has not been raised, our preaching is useless and so is your faith. . . . But Christ has indeed been raised from the dead" (1 Corinthians 15:14, 20, NIV). This truth presents itself clearly in all orthodox statements of faith. The resurrection of Christ is affirmed by churchgoers week after week as various creeds are recited: "For our sake he was crucified under Pontius Pilate; he suffered death and was buried. On the third day he rose again in accordance with the Scriptures." But beyond this glorious truth, the dynamic reality of this risen Christ must come to life among his people. Through their hands and feet and words, the King continues the mind-boggling work of bringing creation back to his original design. The Scriptures say we represent the first fruits of his efforts. At some future time, the full harvest will come in.

All Christians should identify with the King and his grand restoration project. He lives in us and continues his work through a new body, the church. Our presence bears witness to the fact that he is still alive, and one day he will return in power and great glory. The mission of the church is exciting beyond words!

THE MIRACLE TOUCH OF JESUS

What people want when they attend church on weekends is the assurance that Christ is truly alive. They need more than the long and fruitful ministry of a friendly pastor who someday might be gone. They need to know that no matter what human leadership is in place, the risen Christ will continue with his mission. He is the great attraction we offer to the traffic whizzing by, and the church should be doing an incredible business.

That's why it's so important that, as his people, we remain involved in the things Jesus is passionate about. How do we do that? We reach out in his name to the poor. We take up the cause of world missions. We get involved in issues of justice or racial reconciliation. We care for the homeless. We position the church in the places where the Living Christ can still pursue his goal of bringing the world into compliance with his will. And if we stay as close to him as possible, the miracles continue.

The fastest way I know to spark a tired congregation is to have several visitors, or people who have been visited by church members, come to know the miracle touch of Jesus. Let them talk about their new joy and enthusiasm in the Lord. When they share about the collision of their stories and his Story, Christians will quickly remember that Jesus lives.

Let those involved in work at the nursing home report on what Jesus means to the old folks they see. The group that goes each week to the downtown mission dare not talk about their sacrifice or the difficulty of the assignment; instead, they need to make known how they carry with them the conviction that Jesus can restore anything broken. Statistics about what church people have done aren't all that important. "Last year we delivered 162 meals to the elderly." No. Rather, tell what Jesus did as you reached out in his name and gave people reason to hope.

Missionaries have it right when they reveal how ears listen attentively and eyes sparkle when those who never knew someone so wonderful exists hear about Jesus for the first time. "Who are we?" the missionaries ask. "Cheap merchandise, easily broken, not worth a second look?" And then they go on to explain the precious news:

"No. We bear the stamp 'made by God.' That's class! At Creation the Spirit of the Maker was breathed into human beings, giving them great dignity.

"Yes. Like our ancestors before us, we listened to the lie. We failed to live loving God and loving others. We contributed to the world's sorrows, just like everyone else. We fell from the high, privileged position God intended us to enjoy.

"On occasion, everyone sees hints of the beauty this world was created to know, but there are far more reasons to be sad. Few have it good; many more have it bad. If the devil is a liar and a cheat, so are those who have listened to him. They aren't all that easy to live with, either. For most people, life is hard and over too soon. Then what?

"Listen." (And bodies lean forward to be sure they hear every word.)

"No one anywhere had answers like the wise prophet from Galilee. He said there could be a new beginning, a second birth, a time when the Spirit would again be breathed into us. To be born physically is an experience common to everyone. To be born of the Spirit is a miracle reserved for those who bow to Christ's kingship.

"Has anyone told you about the holy elixir? A divine remedy was needed in order to take away the sins of the world. That's why Jesus, God's Son, had to die on the cross. King's blood was the ransom price demanded. Yes. He went ahead and paid it.

"But he rose again! What exciting news! Now we can be forgiven and made innocent and new again. We can be filled with the Spirit of God like back in Eden. We can have a fresh start. We can be lifted to the heights we once knew. This time we can stay close to the Creator and be doubly leery of the devil. We can live loving God and loving others, just like Jesus did. Wouldn't it be something if everyone lived this way? Wouldn't that make the world a better place?

"Do you want to be a King's man or a King's woman? A King's son or a King's daughter? If so, once he lives in you, will you in turn identify with what's important to him? The poor must not be neglected. The broken will need to find the King who cares. Injustice cannot be tolerated. Will you say, 'All I have and all I am I dedicate to His Majesty to use any way he pleases'?"

Tears often fill the eyes of those who hear for the first time such a marvelous message. Numbers respond, and others express an immediate interest to know more.

EVIDENCES OF LIFE

At one time evangelicals in our country kept alive this message of the new birth. In spite of ridicule, they went right on preaching about the need to be born again. Individuals had to be made right before the Lord, and the only way this could happen was through the blood of Jesus. I thank God for their persistence.

Mainline churches saw the need for congregations to address societal issues. Their ears heard Jesus when he put on the prophet's mantle and talked about the plight of the poor and the powerless. They didn't want to repeat the mistake of the Pharisees. They wouldn't be legalistic regarding personal piety only to miss what Jesus called the weightier matters of the Law, such as justice and mercy (Matthew 23:23). I'm glad for their sensitivity as well.

In recent years, charismatics have come out of

nowhere to suddenly be cutting-edge in the churches of this land and around the world. They have made us aware of the multifaceted gifts of Jesus and the Holy Spirit. Visit their churches, and you can't miss the conviction that the Lord lives and is doing a great work in our day. Praise the Lord for their openness to both the new wine and the new wineskins!

I'm a novice in learning about the liturgical arena. But I'm discovering that what I always understood to be symbols can mean something much deeper than I had thought. And I'm not ready to foolishly dismiss lessons learned through the centuries by these Christ-honoring friends. Their time-tested traditions have obviously drawn multitudes to the Living Christ and helped differentiate saints from sinners. So I thank God for them, too.

Evangelical, mainline, charismatic, liturgical—which church is the right one? I'm incapable of answering that. I do know that in all churches *facts* about the risen Christ should be overshadowed by *evidences* that his resurrection life is still touching people in remarkable ways. We need to hear testimonies of changed individuals and to see remarkable demonstrations of the new family of God alive with his love. We must be a church at large that rejoices in *all* efforts being done in the name of Christ, because the job at hand is colossal. He must increase; we must decrease.

If that's not happening, our Lord's been put in a most disadvantaged position. If he has been made to appear small and his work inconsequential, this positioning problem will lead to a host of other difficulties. For example, King's troops will always get tired and may even die out if they put too much thought into *what's in this for me?* When they trust their Commander explicitly and seek in every way to please him, it's amazing how long they can stay happy in their assignments.

Tapped-out Christians and tired churches need to position themselves to experience the miracle touch of the Living Christ. Are new people at your church discovering what it means to once again be elevated to their rightful position? I didn't ask whether "customers" were beating a path to your door. But are there at least some who are tasting the Bread of Life for the first time? I hope so. Seeing a hungry person satisfied does wonders for everyone's energy level. The ambiance of the place reflects enjoyment and enthusiasm when each person involved is suddenly reassured that the food is still great!

> **THE KEY: TAPPED-OUT CHRISTIANS AND TIRED CHURCHES NEED TO POSITION THEMSELVES TO EXPERIENCE THE MIRACLE TOUCH OF THE LIVING CHRIST.**

It's hard to imagine a church where Easter is celebrated but few people ever pass from death to new life. That's like having the secret to working miracles in someone's life while never tapping into it.

Does the King's dream of the better world still fire your imagination? Jesus said we were his model city program. Positioned on a hill, we can't help but be seen. So when others look at us, do they immediately see our love for God and for others? Is Christian hospitality being extended? Are we telling stories of the King's touch? Do the disadvantaged have their needs met as the church scatters—do we represent Christ in this way 24 hours a day, 7 days a week? Is our love for creation as obvious as our love for the Creator? Are we still good caretakers of the earth's resources? Is Christ doing today in his body, the church, the things he did when he walked this earth so many years ago?

Do we have the Living Christ positioned in the best possible way to show others who he is and what he's about? Or have we left him in a place where strangers asking for directs are all but told, "It's kind of hard to get there from here." When the troops are caught up in their various tasks but don't have the big picture clearly in mind anymore, it's little wonder they lose their energy.

WISPS OF GLORY

T. H. White's classic "Once and Future King" was the basis for the immensely popular musical *Camelot*. Most people have heard the songs and have a feel for the story. Arthur's magical kingdom is like an Eden of his own making. The Crown has made it clear that the weather must be perfect all year round. By 8:00 in the morning, the fog must lift. There's a legal limit to how much snow can fall, and so on. In short, there's no "more congenial spot for happily-ever-aftering than here in Camelot."

Arthur dreams of a new and better world order. To pull this off, he invites knights from many countries to sit with him in fellowship and counsel at a great round table. But all comes to naught when the most noble of those in his service, Lancelot of France, has an ongoing affair with Arthur's queen, Guinevere.

In the closing scene of the production, Arthur is alone on stage with a lad the audience hasn't met before. Guinevere has been condemned to the flames. Lancelot has returned from France to attempt a rescue. A great battle is in process, and no one really knows who is winning.

Smoke lifts from the stage, and the king stands in the chaos of his dying kingdom. That's when the young boy makes his entrance. Taken up with the excitement of everything that's happening, and unaware of the great pain involved, he tells King Arthur he wants to be a knight of his famous Round Table. In a tender scene, the king looks at the lad kindly and sings of the tale he's fashioned

> HE TOLD US TO ASK EVERYONE IF THEY'VE HEARD HIS STORY. IF NOT, WE MUST TELL IT STRONG AND CLEAR. IT'S NOT A WISP OF GLORY, BUT AN ONGOING REALITY.

and its better chapters: "Ask every person if he's heard the story, and tell it strong and clear if he has not, that once there was a fleeting wisp of glory—called Camelot."

A fleeting wisp of glory . . . And I choke back tears.

Then I realize I'm not the only one who is having a hard time keeping from crying. My wife, Karen, takes my hand and squeezes it. The man on my right wipes his eyes. This dream of a better world lies deep within the psyche of almost everyone. I'm amazed at how profoundly the audience is touched.

But I have saved the best for last. It's my great privilege to write that there is a living King. He's all you ever wanted him to be and more. To know him is to know what life is all about. And the offer of involvement in his past, present, and future kingship is to be taken seriously. He told us to ask everyone if they've heard his story. If not, we must tell it strong and clear. It's not a wisp of glory, but an ongoing reality to be found anywhere you travel in this world. Christ's kingship stands firm wherever people bow before him as King and live as he taught.

"Your kingdom come, your will be done on earth as it is in heaven," his subjects pray. That's the way he instructed us to speak with our heavenly Father. The words are a reminder that in heaven, all recognize Christ as King and obey his will. Because of this, the beings in his presence reap great benefit. So we ask the Lord to let us live in that same fashion here on earth, where we also recognize him as our sovereign. We put his desires above our own. And the prayer carries with it a belief that the benefits we presently experience are nothing compared to the glories we will someday know.

"Don't let it be forgotten," we say to one another, "that for a brief shining moment there was a special place where our ancestors actually communed with their Creator. They knew his presence walking with them in the cool of the day. Unfortunately that paradise was ruined. But a divine restoration process is going on, and we're an integral part of it.

"To be honest, sometimes work in behalf of the King makes us tired. Then we're reminded of what are incredible truths. This Christ we serve is the one who began everything. When hope was gone, he humbled himself and came to earth so all things broken could be restored. By way of illustration, he continues to do a remarkable job changing each of us. We in turn have impacted our worlds in more ways than we realize. The overall job is not done, but we know some day it will be. Then, 'the end shall come, when he hands over the kingdom to God the Father after he has destroyed all dominion, authority, and power.'

"The Crown has made it clear. That's why tears of gratitude fill our eyes. Of all people in the world, we are the most fortunate. We're actually living the dream of the better world right now, and we will be happily-ever-aftering as well!"

Dr. **David R. Mains** is director of The Chapel Ministries, the non-profit Christian media outreach that has been producing the annual 50-Day Spiritual Adventure since 1980. His much-loved books on spiritual issues and his popularity as a speaker demonstrate people's resounding response to David's greatest desire—to see revival descend upon North America.

He first became known in the Christian community for his work with Circle Church, a pioneering congregation that attracted many who would otherwise have avoided the church in the 1960s. His book *Full Circle* outlines incredible renewal and reconciliation among the hundreds who attended worship services at Circle Church in inner-city Chicago.

In 1977, David began to minister through the Christian media. His primary voice, "The Chapel of the Air" radio broadcast, reached thousands of loyal listeners for two decades. More recently, he has hosted "You Need to Know," a daily television show named 1995 Program of the Year by the National Religious Broadcasters. Currently his TV team, Live Dog Productions, generates videos for Mainstay Church Resources and various other companies.

David Mains and his wife, Karen, have been married for 36 years and live in the western Chicago suburbs. As the parents of four grown children, the Mainses are highly committed to Christian family values and are eagerly sharing their inestimable experience with the next generation, their growing clan of grandchildren.

Thy Kingship Come

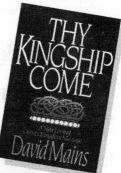

*A New Look at Christ's
Kingdom Message*

by David Mains

Discover for yourself the Jewish
expectation of a great king while explore
the meaning of "kingdom" terms in Scripture. David
Mains's unique perspective on the kingdom of God—
more easily understood as Christ's "kingship"—will
challenge your spiritual life and lead you to a deeper,
more meaningful faith.

If you believe your knowledge of Christ's kingdom or
your understanding of its importance is limited, take
heart. This book was written in an easy-to-read, personal style to help you take a new look at Christ's kingdom message and relate the kingship of Jesus Christ to
your own life.

Come, reacquaint yourself with the King of kings.
Make ready your heart to enthrone him and offer
your life as his kingdom.

Specs: trade paper, 186 pages, $9

*To order, call Mainstay Church Resources toll free at 1-800-
224-2735 or contact your local Christian bookstore.*

The Kingdom Tales Trilogy

by David and Karen Mains

Your entire family will love these delightful stories that communicate vital biblical truths. They're all about boys and girls, men and women who help reestablish the kingdom in a world that rightfully belongs to the King.

In the Gold Medallion Award-winning *Tales of the Kingdom* you'll meet Scarboy, the orphan who escapes the dark and cruel Enchanted City with his brother Little Child. Seeking asylum in Great Park, they meet many fascinating characters, including the King himself, who invites Hero into the Great Celebration's fire-circle that changes his subjects from what they seem to the beautiful persons they really are. Kids of all ages will love these powerful stories, for they have the potential to work their own surprising transformations in a reader's life.

The story continues in another Gold Medallion Award winner, *Tales of the Resistance*. Meet new characters and follow these winsome friends as they search for the King each day in the middle of the dark Enchanted City, and you too will begin to see how God gets involved in your everyday world.

Just released, *Tales of the Restoration* traces the activities of Hero other friends as they begin to restore the kingship in the newly dubbed Bright City. You'll learn valuable lessons about service and spiritual warfare from the way each character empowers one another to use his or her gifts to bring about the loving desires of the King.

Your family will appreciate the deep biblical principles woven throughout every story as you laugh with enjoyment, ache with anticipation, and shiver with excitement for the characters in this trilogy. Order your *Kingdom Tales* copies today!

Specs: full-color illustrated, hard cover casebound, approx. 110 pages each, $19 per book. *Tales of the Resistance* and *Tales of the Restoration* now available.

To order, call Mainstay Church Resources toll free at 1-800-224-2735 or contact your local Christian bookstore.

8 Survival Skills for Changing Times

by David Mains

The world is changing with unprecedented speed. Countries and political systems are splitting up. So are more and more families. Crime is skyrocketing, and the economy can decline just as quickly. And faith in the God of the Bible is fading for almost everyone—Christians included.

How can you keep from being thrown off balance by all this upheaval? David Mains has the answers. He offers you a "life preserver" in the form of eight survival skills—practical strategies to keep your values and your faith intact in changing times.

Change is just as sure as the future is unsure. But you can be confident and secure in an unchanging God and an unshaken faith. This book will help you stay afloat, even in turbulent waters.

Specs: trade paper, 156 pages, $9

To order, call Mainstay Church Resources toll free at 1-800-224-2735 or contact your local Christian bookstore.

When Life Becomes a Maze

Discovering Christ's Resources for Times of Confusion

by David R. Mains

Sooner or later everyone faces a maze. No matter who you are or where you live in the world, life presents labyrinths in finances, job situations, family relationships, and many other areas. So what do you do when you're confused? Well, first of all, don't panic! You can discover Christ's resources for times of confusions, and *When Life Becomes a Maze* will help you do it.

David Mains vulnerably shares the principles he learned while in his own maze. He talks about clinging to God's promises, searching for joys, accepting forgiveness, strengthening your faith, and much more. Plus, special "What to Do" sections at the end of each chapter help you practically, creatively implement in your personal life the suggestions found in this book.

When Life Becomes a Maze is full of hope. No matter what puzzling perplexity you're face, it offers assurance that you too can make it through life's mazes with the Lord by your side.

Available in book or audio cassette format

Specs: mass market, 173 pages, $6, audiobook $12

Getting Beyond "How Are You?"

Learning to Connect in a Disconnected World

by David Mains and
Melissa Mains Timberlake

Why do so many of us have difficulty getting past surface conversations, especially when we long for more meaningful relationships?

David Mains and Melissa Mains Timberlake provide the vital key to making substantive, meaningful connections with others: asking good questions. When we learn to uncover answers that get beyond facts to feelings and beyond feelings to the heart of another person, we can touch lives with the love of Christ.

Getting Beyond "How Are You?" is a short, easy-to-read handbook packed with ideas on how to really reach others. Appropriate as a study guide for small groups or Christian education classes, each chapter has questions to help you and other friends examine and apply what you've learned in practical ways.

Do you long for closer relationships with others at church, at home, at work, in social gatherings, or wherever you go? Let David Mains and Melissa Mains Timberlake lead you from small talk to deep, significant, life-healing conversation.

Specs: mass market, 105 pages, $4

To order, call Mainstay Church Resources toll free at 1-800-224-2735 or contact your local Christian bookstore.

Two Are Better Than One

A Guide to Prayer
Partnerships That Work
by David Mains & Steve Bell

This step-by-step guide for setting up your own prayer partnership will enable you to:

• Experience the power of God at work in your life
• Develop enduring friendships
• Increase your ability to resist temptation
• Sense God's special concern and care for you

Written by The Chapel of the Air Ministries director David Mains and Steve Bell, executive director of Concerts of Prayer International, this little primer includes hints on how to set up a prayer partnership and ways to organize and keep track of prayer requests and answers. It also holds a myriad of Scripture verses to share with your prayer partner as together you communicate with God to conquer difficulties that come your way, bringing energy and renewal to your spiritual life.

Specs: mass market, 134 pages, $5

To order, call Mainstay Church Resources toll free at 1-800-224-2735 or contact your local Christian bookstore.

The Sense of His Presence

Experiencing Classic Revival
by David Mains

According to David Mains, revival always holds an overwhelming sense of Christ's presence. And when people feel that presence, eight fundamental things take place—true worship, great love for one another, a desire to be holy, an eagerness to serve, hunger for God's Word, boldness in prayer, outreaching evangelism, a sense of well-being. When these factors are present, we can be sure the church is functioning as Christ intended. We can also be sure revival is in process!

With its built-in study guide and resourceful excerpts from other writers, this book is an invaluable exploration of how Christians can prepare for revival. *The Sense of His Presence* offers a vivid and compelling picture of the Christian life at its best, the life lived in full awareness that Christ is here.

Specs: trade paper, 192 pages, $9

To order, call Mainstay Church Resources toll free at 1-800-224-2735—or contact your local Christian bookstore or church book table.

Living, Loving, Leading

*Creating a home that
encourages spiritual growth*

by David & Karen Mains

Why do thousands of Christians seem so
dissatisfied with the spiritual conditions of their own
homes? Part of our problem, say David and Karen
Mains, is that we're not sure what spiritual leadership
looks like. We have problems fleshing it out because
we can't see it.

Living, Loving, Leading offers a tangible, "seeable"
model for encouraging your family's spiritual develop-
ment. Join David and Karen as they suggest some
helpful, biblical ideas for raising the spiritual temper-
ature of your home. Walk with them as they describe
their own struggles and triumphs, and as they search
for workable solutions to the crucial question, "How
can we become spiritual leaders of our family?"

You can create a home that encourages spiritual
growth! Can you afford to wait any longer?

Specs: cloth, 244 pages, $11

Reversing Self-Destructive Patterns

Maybe it's worry, a short temper, perfectionism. Whatever "it" happens to be, you know it's self-destructive and it simply has to stop. Soon!

With the help of this book, it can. *Reversing Self-Destructive Patterns* is a hands-on, reader-involving, Bible-based guide that walks you through the process of reversing the habits that hurt you. It teaches you step by step to start charting your behavior, analyzing the patterns, and creating practical strategies toward change.

Created by The Chapel of the Air Ministries, this short book is designed specifically for those who want to deal with their dysfunctional—or just plain annoying—habits. *Reversing Self-Destructive Patterns* is sure to alter your mind and spirit, enabling you to enjoy new and healthy ways of living.

Specs: mass market, 94 pages, $4

To order, call Mainstay Church Resources toll free at 1-800-224-2735 or contact your local Christian bookstore.

When the Troops Are Tired

The Audiobook!

How often have you wished, "If only I had more time to read!" Here's your chance to discover and re-discover all the benefits of this book without giving up precious time. This cassette recording of *When the Troops Are Tired* will help you fit quality learning time right into your schedule while commuting to work, chauffeuring kids, exercising—whenever you have a chance to listen while doing!

David Mains's more than 20-year experience in broadcasting "The Chapel of the Air" 15-minute radio show, as well as his extensive speaking and interviewing background, have contributed to making this two-tape series a first-class product.

The book will become all the more meaningful as you hear David's memorable stories and practical advice from his own lips. You're sure to enjoy his delightful expression and easy-to-listen-to voice as he rallies Christ's troops and infuses your own life with more spiritual energy.

Specs: approx. 180 minutes, $13

To order, call Mainstay Church Resources toll free at 1-800-224-2735—or contact your local Christian bookstore or church book table.